W9-AWW-978

THE FRONTIER

Everyday Life:

WALTER A. HAZEN

Good Year Books

An Imprint of Addison-Wesley Educational Publishers, Inc.

Photo Credits

Unless otherwise credited, all photographs are the property of Addison-Wesley Educational Publishers, Inc. Front Cover: Frontier family in front of covered wagons: Colorado Historical Society; California land ad: New-York Historical Society; p.3 Newberry Library, Edward E. Ayer Collection; p.4 Denver Public Library; p.5 Union Pacific Museum Collection; p.10 Kansas State Historical Society, Topeka; p.11 Oregon Historical Society; p.12, 13 Kansas State Historical Society, Topeka; p.18 Solomon D. Butcher Collection/Nebraska State Historical Society; p.19 Courtesy John Hancock Mutual Life Insurance Company; p.20 State Historical Society of Colorado; p.21 Courtesy, Levi Strauss & Company; p.26 Kansas State Historical Society, Topeka; p.27 State Historical Society of Wisconsin; p.29 Linton Park, "Flax Scutching Bee," National Gallery of Art, Washington, D.C., Gift of Edgar William and Bernice Chrysler Garbisch; p.34 Kansas State Historical Society, Topeka; p.35 Library of Congress; p.36, 37 Kansas State Historical Society, Topeka; p.42 Corbis-Bettmann; p.43 National Archives; p.44 Kansas State Historical Society, Topeka; p.45 Solomon D. Butcher Collection/Nebraska State Historical Society; p.50 Corbis-Bettmann ; p.51 Kansas State Historical Society, Topeka; p.52 California Historical Society; p.58 California State Library; p.60 Culver Pictures Inc.; p.61(t) Arizona Historical Society; p.61(b) Kansas State Historical Society, Topeka; p.66(b) Wichita Public Library; p.67 Local History Section/Wichita Public Library; p.69(t) Kansas State Historical Society, Topeka; p.69(b) Santa Fe Railway Photo; p.71 Montana Historical Society; p.75 Western History Collections, University of Oklahoma Library ; p.76 Denver Public Library; p.77 Library of Congress; p.82 Kansas State Historical Society, Topeka; p.83 Courtesy of the New-York Historical Society; p.84 Robert Lindneux, "Trail of Tears," Woolaroc Museum, Bartesville, Oklahoma; p.85(b) Smithsonian Institution; p.85(t) Kansas State Historical Society, Topeka

Check out these other books in the *Everyday Life* series from Good Year Books, including

Everyday Life: **Colonial Times**

Everyday Life: **Inventions**

Everyday Life: **The Civil War**

Coming Spring of 1999

Everyday Life: **Transportation**

Everyday Life: **Reconstruction to 1900**

Dedication

To Martha, Jordan, and Allison

Acknowledgments

Grateful acknowledgment is extended to my editor, Laura Strom, who has guided me through several books in Good Year's "Everyday Life" series. Without her advice and support, this book would not have been possible.

I would also like to thank Roberta Dempsey, Editorial Director at Good Year, for giving me the opportunity to be a part of such an exciting project. Her support and confidence in me is likewise appreciated.

Good Year Books

are available for most basic curriculum subjects plus many enrichment areas. For more Good Year Books, contact your local bookseller or educational dealer. For a complete catalog with information about other Good Year Books, please write to:

Good Year Books
1900 East Lake Avenue
Glenview, Illinois 60025

Design: Ronan Design

Silhouette Illustrations: Joe Rogers

Copyright © 1999 Good Year Books,
    an imprint of Addison-Wesley Educational Publishers Inc.

All Rights Reserved.

Printed in the United States of America.

ISBN 0-673-36405-4

1 2 3 4 5 6 7 8 9 - BW - 06 05 04 03 02 01 00 99 98

Only portions of this book intended for classroom use may be reproduced without permission in writing from the publisher.

Table of Contents

From *Everyday Life: The Frontier* © 1999 Good Year Books.

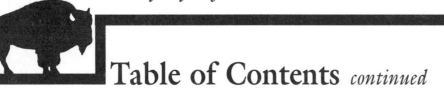
Table of Contents *continued*

From *Everyday Life: The Frontier* © 1999 Good Year Books.

Introduction

The Frontier. The West. The Old West. The Wild West. The Far West. The Last Frontier. By whatever name it was called as it advanced to the Pacific Ocean, the story of the American frontier is one of excitement and adventure.

The word *frontier* can loosely be defined as where settlements end and the wilds begin. The first frontier in America extended from the Atlantic Ocean to the Appalachian Mountains. Until 1763, only a few hunters and trappers had ventured beyond this natural border. But, in time, some of the 3,000,000 English colonists who lived along the Atlantic Seaboard began to grow restless. Natural curiosity and the desire for more fertile lands caused the adventuresome among them to look west for a better way of life.

In 1763, following the French and Indian War, Great Britain gained control of French lands between the Appalachian Mountains and the Mississippi River. King George III immediately declared the area off-limits to settlement, preferring not to stir up the Indians who lived there. But some colonists ignored his command and, about the year 1770, began making their way into the wilderness. Five years later, Daniel Boone and a company of men blazed the Wilderness Road through a gap in the mountains and opened the gateway to the West. In a short time, settlers began to pour through the Appalachians into the Mississippi and Ohio valleys. They established the second American frontier, which centered around what are now the states of Ohio, Kentucky, Tennessee, Indiana, and Illinois. Other pioneers made their way into the upper Great Lakes and Gulf of Mexico regions.

By the 1830s, most of the land east of the Mississippi River had been settled. Pioneers then pushed across the Great Plains and the Rocky Mountains to Utah, California, and Oregon. In May 1841, the first of many pioneer wagon trains left Missouri and headed across the continent to the Pacific. Nearly all passed through the dry and treeless plains, which at the time were considered unfit for settlement.

The final frontier in America began after the Civil War with the settlement of the Great Plains. For a period of about thirty years, farmers, ranchers, and miners flocked to the area. Many of these pioneers were immigrants from Europe. The frontier is said to have ended in 1890 with the final subjugation (conquest) of the American Indians and the fencing-in of the open range.

Walter A. Hazen

From Everyday Life: The Frontier © 1999 Good Year Books.

CHAPTER 1

The Frontier: Getting There

As illustrated in a painting by artist John Gast, Americans of the 19th century believed it was the "Manifest Destiny" of the United States to expand all the way to the Pacific.

The first pioneers who struck out across the Appalachian Mountains traveled by foot and horseback. Most followed Daniel Boone's Wilderness Road, which ran some 300 miles from Virginia to Kentucky and then on to Ohio. A few crossed the mountains farther north along what was called the Mohawk Trail.

Travel along the Wilderness Road was difficult and dangerous. In its early years, the road was little more than a path cut through the thick forest and undergrowth. Trees that bordered the road were notched so pioneers who followed it could find their way. When travelers came to a stream, they either swam or waded across, or stopped and built a raft. At night, they slept on the ground, covering themselves with animal furs. There was always the danger of hostile Indians, who resented the white man's encroachment on their lands.

In spite of the hardships, about 200,000 settlers had traveled the Wilderness Road by the end of the 18th century. Later, the road was widened to accommodate wagons, and it eventually matched the Ohio River as one of the great highways to the West.

As the frontier pushed ever westward, there was a demand for more roads. The first, completed in 1794, was called the Lancaster Turnpike. Built of crushed rock and gravel, it ran from Philadelphia to Lancaster, Pennsylvania, a distance of about 60 miles. Over the next few years, similar roads were built that connected the cities of the East with settlements on the frontier. Over these roads traveled pioneers in Conestoga wagons loaded with their belongings. First built in the Conestoga Valley of Pennsylvania (and hence the name), these wagons had large wheels that prevented them from sinking in the mud that was characteristic of early roads.

The first national road was built in 1811. It ran 600 miles from Cumberland, Maryland, to Vandalia, Illinois, not far from the Mississippi River. First known as the Cumberland Road, its name was later changed to the National Road. Over it passed thousands of pioneers in covered wagons and stagecoaches. Others plodded along on horseback or on foot. (One family of

From *Everyday Life: The Frontier* © 1999 Good Year Books.

seven was observed walking from New Jersey to Ohio, pushing their worldly possessions along in a wheelbarrow.) At its western conclusion, the National Road hooked up with the river traffic of the Ohio and Mississippi rivers. From there the pioneers continued their journey by water.

Travel downstream on one of the rivers leading west or south was usually by flatboat. A flatboat was a large raft with a flat bottom, square ends, and high sides. It was steered and partially propelled by one or two long oars. One oar was located at the rear of the boat. The other was situated atop a boxlike house built in the center. The house provided shelter from the elements and some protection from Indians, who sometimes attacked the boats while they were tied up at night. Flatboats were large enough to carry an entire family with all their furniture and livestock.

Travel down the river by flatboat was dangerous. Not only did those who worked on the boats ("river men") have to look out for hostile Indians, but also for sandbars, snags, and changing currents as well. Many flatboats were sunk by sudden storms, and pioneers watched helplessly as their furniture and belongings plunged to the bottom of the river.

But river travel could also be fun. River men were rough-talking frontiersmen who kept travelers entertained with their high jinks and stories. Many flatboats had an official fiddler, whose only job was to play for the passengers. As the boat slowly made its way downstream, women busied themselves with cooking and sewing, while children passed the time fishing and swimming. A trip down the river to a settlement in the West might take up to three months.

Once a flatboat reached its destination, it was dismantled and sold for lumber or firewood. This was done because the large crafts could not travel back upstream against the current. If the pioneers aboard the boat happened to own it (some sold their wagons and bought their own boats), they took it apart and used the boards to help build their first home. River men who had steered them downstream had to find other means of transportation back

Pioneers steer their flatboat down the Ohio River. The flatboat was a principal means of river travel until the advent of the steamboat.

home. Many who could not afford the price of a stagecoach or steamboat ticket simply walked.

Flatboats were slowly replaced by steamboats and by barges that traveled on the Erie Canal and other canals. But in their heyday, these practical vessels jammed the rivers that led to the western settlements. In 1846 alone, more than 2,000 flatboats sailed down the Mississippi River to New Orleans.

When the lands bordering the Mississippi became crowded and settlers set their sights beyond the Rocky Mountains to California and Oregon, a new means of travel appeared: the prairie schooner. The prairie schooner was a smaller relative of the Conestoga wagon used in the East. It was so-named because, when viewed from a distance while traveling on the prairie, its white canvas top resembled the sail of a ship.

Pioneers traveled west on two main trails, the Oregon Trail and the Santa Fe Trail. The most important was the Oregon Trail, which ran for about 2,400 miles (about 3,900 km) from Independence, Missouri, to the Pacific Northwest. When the trail passed through the opening in the Rocky Mountains known as South Pass, it divided. One branch (later known as the Overland Trail) continued on toward Oregon. The other led through the deserts of Utah and Nevada to central California. This second branch, called the California Trail, was used largely by pioneers caught up in the gold rush of 1849.

The Santa Fe Trail, which also began in Independence, Missouri, ran for 780 miles (1,255 km) to Santa Fe, New Mexico, and was used by pioneers to reach the Southwest. An extension of the Santa Fe Trail called the Old Spanish Trail wound its way in a semicircular route from Santa Fe to Los Angeles, California.

Independence, Missouri, on the Missouri River, was the "jumping off" point for pioneers traveling west. At Independence, wagons gathered to be formed into wagon trains. Most pioneers traveled in prairie schooners, but

A long wagon train winds it way over Ute Pass in Colorado. Such trains carried vital supplies to settlers in remote Western areas.

there were some who traveled along in simple farm wagons. Others had no wagons at all. Many of the Mormons who migrated to the Great Salt Lake Valley of Utah walked, pushing or pulling their possessions in two-wheeled carts.

Wagon trains usually left Independence in late April or early May. The trip took about six months, and, if all went well, the wagons would clear the Rocky Mountains before the winter blizzards set in. The early weeks of the journey were the most pleasant. The weather was good, and the oxen pulling the wagons were fresh and still strong. People were in high spirits as they talked and dreamed of the new life ahead of them.

On a good day, a wagon train might make twenty miles. Each day began before sunrise and continued until sunset. Everyone was up by 5 A.M. and on the trail by 7 A.M. At noon, the wagon train stopped just long enough for the animals to rest and the people to eat. It then continued on until late afternoon, when the day's journey ended. Before darkness set in, the wagons formed a large circle for protection against the possibility of Indian attack. Inside this circle, campfires were started and an evening meal of beans, dried buffalo meat, and journeycake was prepared. Children ran excitedly from campfire to campfire,

playing tag and other games. After dinner, a fiddler sometimes played and people danced. But the evening's activities ended early. Morning came all too soon, and another hard day on the trail could be anticipated.

As the wagon train continued along each day, only women, young children, and people who were sick or injured rode in the wagons. The men and boys walked. Boys also had the responsibility of watching the herd of cows, beef cattle, and extra oxen that followed to the rear of the train. When the train stopped each day for lunch, one chore of the younger children was to fan out across the prairie and gather buffalo chips (manure) for the evening fires.

Engines from the Union Pacific and Central Pacific Railroads meet at Promontory Point, Utah, on May 10, completing the construction of the transcontinental railroad.

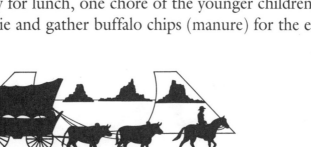

Movies usually depict wagon trains as being under constant attack by hostile Indians. This simply was not the case. There were, to be sure, Indian attacks from time to time, and people were killed. But a far greater number of pioneers died from other causes. Cholera and typhoid caused the deaths of thousands, and the trails heading west were marked with their graves. People drowned in swollen streams and died from snakebites. Children sometimes fell from wagons and were crushed under the wheels of the wagons that followed. Others were killed in cattle stampedes set off by lightning and thunder. Sources estimate that one out of every seventeen pioneers who set out from Missouri was buried along the Oregon Trail.

Those pioneers who did make it all the way to California or Oregon usually arrived with the barest of necessities: possibly a few pots and pans, some tools, and their clothes. Many had left Independence with wagons carrying large pieces of furniture, fine china, and other treasures, but these items had to be abandoned along the way to make the wagons light enough to climb the mountains. Alongside grave markers and the bleached bones of oxen who had died on the trail from exhaustion, wagon trains that followed found massive oak dressers and ornate tables scorching in the desert sun.

With the settling of Oregon and California, there remained only one large area of the frontier left to be conquered. That was the Great Plains, or the area between the Mississippi River and the Rocky Mountains. Originally designated as "Indian Country," the plains were for years considered unsuitable for farming. Americans referred to the vast area as the "Great American Desert."

Two events sparked renewed interest in the plains. In 1862, the Homestead Act offered 160 acres to any pioneer who would agree to settle and live on the land for five years. Several "runs" were staged where settlers in wagons lined up and, at a given signal, raced to claim the best acreage. Ranchers and cowboys also flocked to the area because of its grazing capabilities.

A second significant event occurred in 1869. Tracks of the Union Pacific and Central Pacific railroads were joined at Promontory Point, Utah, completing the first transcontinental railroad. Over these tracks came thousands of immigrants from Europe to establish homesteads on the prairie. By 1890, the Great Plains had been settled, and the American frontier came to an end.

From *Everyday Life: The Frontier* © 1999 Good Year Books.

Name _____ Date _____

Keep a Covered Wagon Diary

Imagine yourself traveling with a wagon train bound for Oregon Country.

Make up a diary entry depicting events that might have occurred during a three-day period on the trail.

Dear Diary,   *July 10–12, 1844*

From Everyday Life: The Frontier © 1999 Good Year Books.

Name _____ Date _____

Complete a Map of Pioneer Trails

On the map provided, label and draw lines to indicate the Oregon Trail, the California Trail, the Santa Fe Trail, and the Old Spanish Trail. Also label on the map the following: California, New Mexico Territory, Utah Territory, Oregon Territory, Independence (Missouri), the Rocky Mountains, South Pass, Santa Fe (New Mexico), Salt Lake City, San Diego, Los Angeles, and San Francisco.

For your research, consult an encyclopedia or any book on the West or the Western frontier.

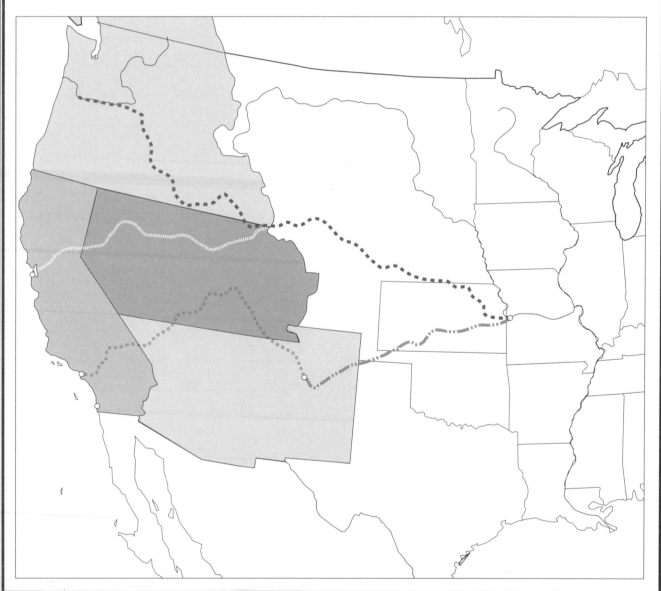

Name _____ Date _____

Interpret a Bar Graph

The Oregon Trail was the longest route used by pioneers to reach the Western frontier. It wound its way some 2,400 miles from Independence, Missouri, to Fort Vancouver in the Oregon Territory.

But there were other routes followed by settlers in their migrations west. The graph on this page shows five of these and the approximate distances they covered.

Use the graph to answer the questions below.

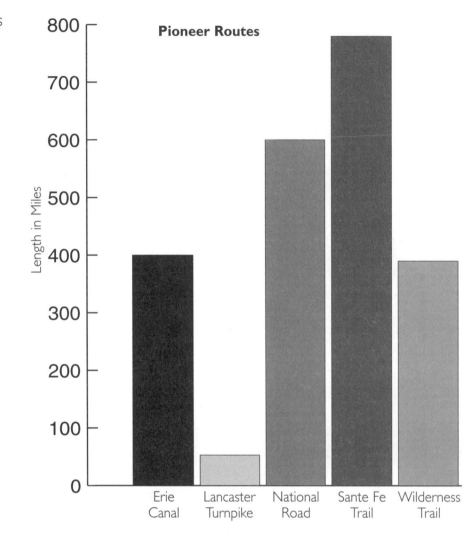

1. What is the total mileage covered by the five routes together? _____ miles

2. What is the mean, or average, distance covered by the routes? _____ miles

3. What is the range? _____ miles

4. Is there a mode? If so, what is it? _____

5. How many times longer was the National Road than the Lancaster Turnpike? _____

6. How much longer was the Santa Fe Trail than the Wilderness Road? _____ miles

From Everyday Life: The Frontier ©1999 Good Year Books.

CHAPTER 2

Frontier Homes

The first order of business for pioneers after reaching their destination was devising some kind of temporary shelter until a permanent home could be built. In the Southwest, where temperatures were milder, pioneers simply lived out of their wagons while building their homes. In colder climates, something a little warmer was needed. Temporary shelters included such structures as Indian-type wigwams, lean-tos or half-faced camps, and dugouts. What one built depended on the weather and the materials at hand.

Pioneers who settled in wooded areas almost always built a lean-to as their first "home." A lean-to was a simple shelter left open on one side. It was easy to build and could be put up rather quickly. First, a crosspole was placed between two small, forked trees spaced the desired distance apart. Then a heavy log was banked with dirt to form a low back wall. From this log to the crosspole, the pioneer laid poles, forming a slanted roof that was covered with bark and branches. The sides of the lean-to were filled in with short poles stuck into the ground. The lean-to always faced south to offer a measure of protection from wind and rain. A fire was kept going constantly before the open side for warmth and to keep wild animals at bay. Some lean-tos, or half-faced, camps were little more than wigwams open on one side, while others were sturdy structures made of logs. Pioneers lived in these rough shelters while they put in their first crop and began work on a log cabin.

Those pioneers who settled on the treeless plains dug shelters into the sides of hills. Such dugouts served as homes until more comfortable sod houses could be built. A dugout was dark and cramped, and impossible to keep clean. But it had an even more unattractive feature. Since it was carved out of a hillside and thus had a natural sod roof, there was always the danger of a grazing cow crashing through at any time. (Bet you never had one of those drop in for dinner!)

A family stands in front of their sod dugout home in Kansas. Such dugouts were usually temporary until a more permanent "soddy" could be built.

14

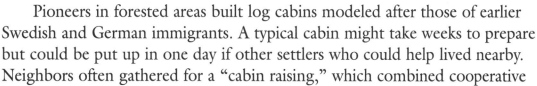

Pioneers in forested areas built log cabins modeled after those of earlier Swedish and German immigrants. A typical cabin might take weeks to prepare but could be put up in one day if other settlers who could help lived nearby. Neighbors often gathered for a "cabin raising," which combined cooperative work with a chance to socialize and have fun. But a lone pioneer, if necessary, could build a cabin by himself using only an ax. It just took him a little longer.

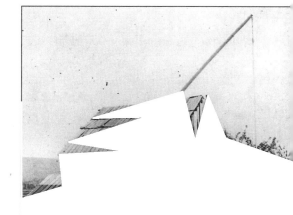

After a sufficient number of tall, straight trees were located and cut down, pioneers rolled or dragged them to the chosen cabin site. There they were cut into lengths of 12 to 18 feet. The logs had to be about the same size in circumference so that the cracks between them could be easily filled. Logs were notched at both ends to ensure that they fit snugly together.

Before the walls were raised, four logs were laid to form a foundation. Most early cabins did not have floors, but those that did had floors made of puncheons. Puncheons were logs split and laid with the flat side up. Every effort was made to smooth the logs to reduce the risk of splinters.

An early ranch house in Eastern Oregon.

As the walls of the cabins went up, openings were cut for windows, a door, and a fireplace. Since glass was not available on the frontier, windows were covered with animal skins or oiled paper. At first the door of a cabin might be an old quilt or hide. Later, a permanent door was made of planks and held in place by leather hinges. A simple lock was made by attaching a string to the latch. The string hung outside the door through a hole. When the string was pulled, it lifted the latch inside and the door could be opened. At night, the string was pulled inside to securely "lock" the door.

Early fireplaces had what were called chimneys. They were made of stacked logs and insulated with "cats," blocks made from mixing mud or clay with grass or pine needles. Cats reduced the danger of fire somewhat, but log chimneys were always a fire threat and could easily burst into flames. As soon as possible, a pioneer family tried to replace their log chimney and fireplace with one made of stone.

Once the walls were completed, the cracks between the logs were chinked, or filled, with mud or clay to keep out the cold winds. Sometimes the mud and clay were mixed with moss, sticks, or small stones to make the

From *Everyday Life: The Frontier* © 1999 Good Year Books.

chinking material more solid. Then a roof was added of overlapping shingles, called shakes, cut with an ax and laid across poles. Since early pioneers had no nails, the shakes were held in place by weight poles and wooden pins.

Early frontier cabins contained little furniture. There might be a table, a few benches, and maybe a cradle. Tables and benches were made from puncheons, and sometimes a bed was built into one cabin wall. Many pioneers never bothered to build a bed at all. They simply wrapped up in an animal skin or blanket and slept on the floor. The more industrious constructed a loft that could be reached by a ladder.

The typical house on the prairie was the sod house. Settlers called it the "soddy," and it satisfied the need for housing on the treeless plains. A sod house was made entirely of large blocks cut from sod, which is grass with its roots and dirt attached. Even the roof was made of sod laid across poles cut from the little wood that was available.

A man and his wife pose outside their sod house in Kansas. It was a common practice for pioneers to have their pictures taken with all or some of their worldly possessions displayed outside.

To build their house, a prairie family cut large, rectangular blocks of sod about six inches thick. It usually took an acre of sod to build a one-room house measuring 16' × 20'. Each block weighed about fifty pounds and was carried to the building site in a wagon. To form the walls, the blocks were stacked like bricks with the grass side down. Any gaps were filled in with dirt or mud. As with the log cabin, openings were left for windows and doors. Homesteaders who could afford them ordered real windows and doors through mail-order catalogs. Most people, however, fashioned these enclosures out of box crates they had brought along on their journey to the frontier.

Sod houses had very definite advantages and disadvantages. On the plus side, they were cozy and warm in the winter and cool as a cave during the summer. They were fireproof, windproof, flaming-arrowproof, and, for the most part, bulletproof. Houses of sod that took about a week to build might last ten years. They could withstand tornadoes and prairie fires, and some are still standing today. Even after lumber became available to homesteaders, many loved their soddies so much that they stayed in them.

From *Everyday Life: The Frontier* © 1999 Good Year Books.

The disadvantages of sod houses were numerous. They were damp and musty, and they leaked when it rained. Children were kept busy protecting bedding from getting wet during rainstorms, as they scurried about with pails trying to catch all the water dripping from the ceiling. Entire meals would be ruined when muddy dirt fell into what was cooking on the stove. Sometimes soup or stew cooked while one of the children held an umbrella over the pot!

Another drawback of soddies was that more than just rainwater sometimes fell from the roof. At any moment, an insect, a rat, or a snake could drop in unannounced. These and other unwelcome guests also managed to tunnel their way through the walls of the house. Some pioneers partially solved this problem by tacking cheesecloth to the rafters of the roof to help catch whatever might tumble down.

In spite of the hardships, homesteaders made sod houses as comfortable as possible. They plastered the walls with a mixture of lime and sand and decorated them with brightly colored gingham cloth. In time, many pioneers covered their hard dirt floors with carpets or animal skins. Some even planted flower seeds on the roof of their soddies to make them more appealing. When these flowers bloomed, along with the prairie roses and morning glories that might spring up on their own, the soddies must have presented a colorful sight to a passer-by.

Many sod houses were sparsely furnished, especially those of hunters, trappers, and newly arrived farmers. There might be a table, a few chairs or benches, and several rough beds. But pictures have survived that show some sod homes furnished with lace curtains, ornate dressers and sideboards, fancy beds, organs, and framed pictures. It all depended on one's means.

As time passed, lumber, brick, and stone became more available on the frontier. This was true even when the boundary stopped at the Mississippi River. By 1810, some pioneers east of the Mississippi had abandoned their log cabins for more elaborate homes. Settlers on the Great Plains did the same with their soddies. But for many years, the log cabin and the soddy were symbolic of life on the American frontier. Without these first, inexpensive homes, settlers could not have withstood the hardships of pioneer life.

Settlers with means often furnished their sod houses with the best the East could offer. Do you think there was room left for the family in this soddy?

From Everyday Life: The Frontier © 1999 Good Year Books.

Name _____ Date _____

Fill in a Venn Diagram

Fill in the Venn diagram with facts about log cabins and sod houses. List features common to both where the circles overlap.

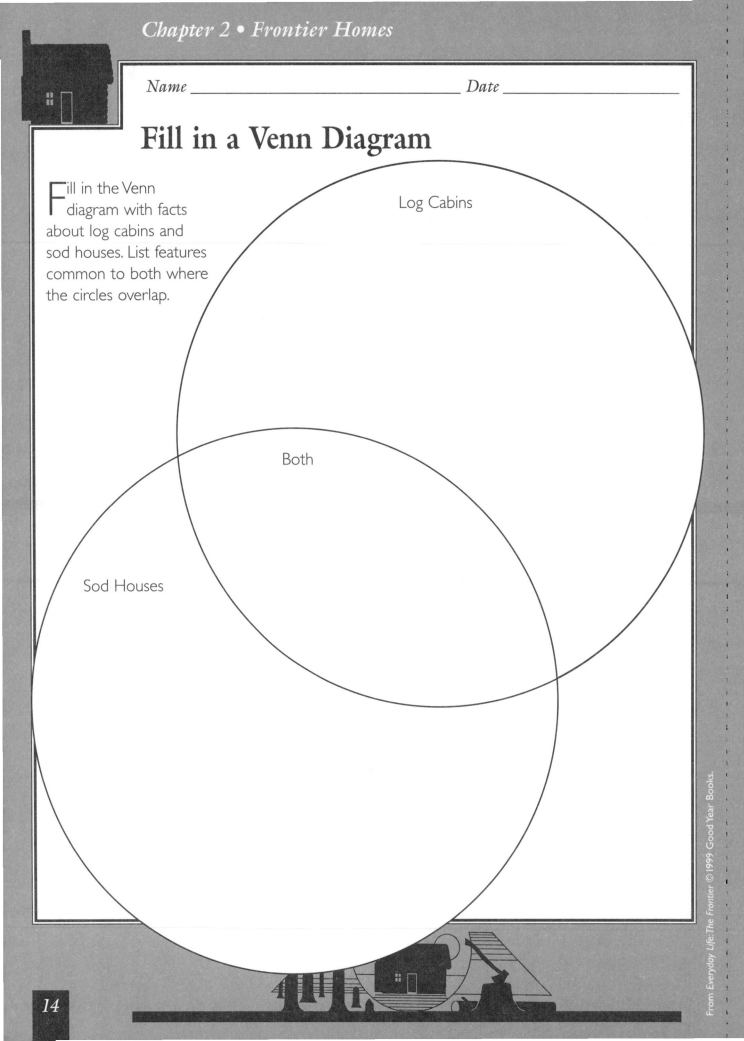

Log Cabins

Both

Sod Houses

From *Everyday Life: The Frontier* © 1999 Good Year Books.

Name _____ Date _____

Make a Shoebox Diorama

Make a shoebox diorama of a scene centered around a log cabin or a sod house. Your diorama might depict one of the following:

1. Men and boys felling trees to build a cabin

2. A family carrying blocks of sod in a wagon to their half-built sod house

3. Men and boys stacking logs to make a cabin wall

4. A plains family sitting in front of their sod house

5. A family eating at a rough table made of puncheons

Or, you may want to think of another scene to create. If you are especially talented and energetic, you might want to make a model of a log cabin or a sod house.

Some materials that will be helpful in preparing your diorama are

1. a large shoebox

2. modeling clay or small figurines

3. construction paper

4. cardboard

5. magic markers or watercolors and paintbrush

6. scissors

7. glue

8. sticks cut into miniature logs

On the lines below, write a brief description of what is being depicted in your diorama.

_____

_____

_____

_____

_____

From Everyday Life: The Frontier ©1999 Good Year Books.

Name _____ Date _____

Write a Letter About a Sod House

Imagine that you have recently arrived on the prairie with your parents and your four younger brothers and sisters. After a long, difficult journey from Ohio and several more weeks devoted to building a sod house, you and your family are at last ready to settle down. On your very first night in the one-room soddy, a heavy rainstorm sweeps across the prairie.

On the lines, write a letter to a former schoolmate in Ohio relating your impressions of the frontier and your thoughts about living in a house made of sod.

Date _____

Dear _____,

_____
_____
_____
_____
_____
_____
_____
_____
_____
_____
_____
_____
_____
_____
_____
_____
_____
_____
_____
_____
_____

Your friend,

_____

From *Everyday Life: The Frontier* © 1999 Good Year Books.

Name _____ Date _____

Use Context Clues to Complete Sentences

Fill in the sentences with the verbs from the word box.

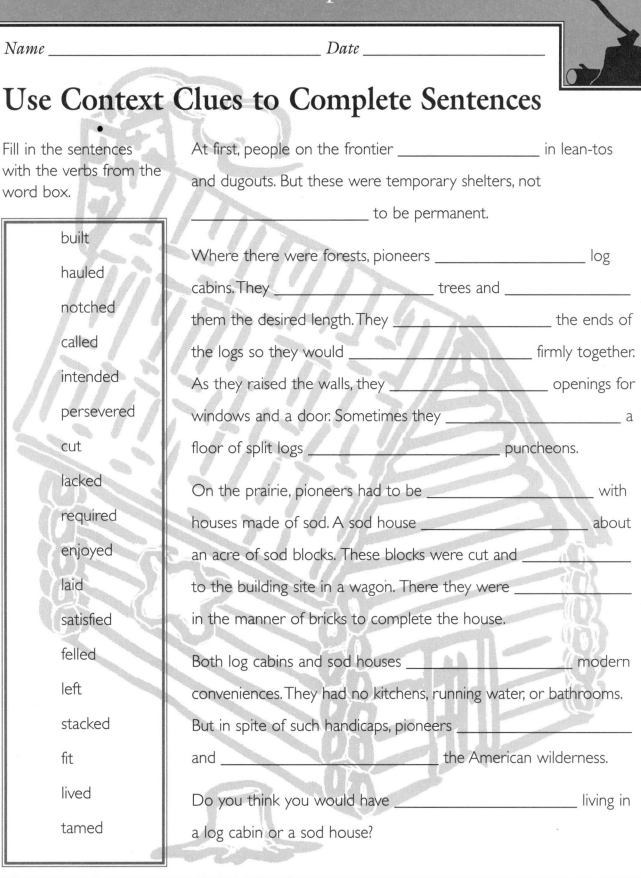

built

hauled

notched

called

intended

persevered

cut

lacked

required

enjoyed

laid

satisfied

felled

left

stacked

fit

lived

tamed

At first, people on the frontier _____ in lean-tos and dugouts. But these were temporary shelters, not _____ to be permanent.

Where there were forests, pioneers _____ log cabins. They _____ trees and _____ them the desired length. They _____ the ends of the logs so they would _____ firmly together. As they raised the walls, they _____ openings for windows and a door. Sometimes they _____ a floor of split logs _____ puncheons.

On the prairie, pioneers had to be _____ with houses made of sod. A sod house _____ about an acre of sod blocks. These blocks were cut and _____ to the building site in a wagon. There they were _____ in the manner of bricks to complete the house.

Both log cabins and sod houses _____ modern conveniences. They had no kitchens, running water, or bathrooms. But in spite of such handicaps, pioneers _____ and _____ the American wilderness.

Do you think you would have _____ living in a log cabin or a sod house?

CHAPTER 3

Food and Clothing

Before pioneers built a permanent shelter, they cleared the land and put in their first crop. Usually this was corn grown from seeds they had brought with them.

A farm couple plow their cornfield in front of their sod house in Nebraska in 1888.

Corn remained the staple crop of pioneers throughout the frontier period. When dried, it was pounded into cornmeal and used to make a wide range of dishes. A kind of cornbread called johnnycake (originally called journeycake) was baked and taken by pioneers when they traveled from place to place. Hoecakes cooked over a griddle, mush, and corn pone were other favorites made from cornmeal. Pone was a kind of cornbread made without milk or eggs but with strips of bacon thrown in.

Besides corn, pioneers grew such vegetables as beans, turnips, squash, cabbage, potatoes, and pumpkins. Vegetables were mixed with pork, venison, or other meat and cooked in a large iron pot over an open fire. When dumplings were added to what was in the pot, the result was a very tasty potpie. Potpies were the staple fare at such community gatherings as house-raisings and quilting bees.

Pioneers supplemented their diet by gathering nuts, berries, wild grapes, and other fruits. On the early frontier, the woods teemed with wild game. Squirrels, rabbits, turkeys, geese, and ducks often found their way onto the pioneer table. The same was true of deer and even bear. Later, a pioneer might keep hogs, a cow, sheep, and some chickens. Chickens were kept for eggs and were rarely eaten.

One staple that was scarce on the frontier was salt. Pioneers who lived near a saline, or salty spring, boiled the water for the salt it provided. Other settlers walked miles to find a salt lick. A salt lick is a rock of salt situated above the ground. It is called a "lick" because deer and other wild animals lick the rock to satisfy their need for salt. Pioneers always collected enough salt from a salt lick to last them a year.

Sugar and coffee were also in short supply on the frontier, especially in the early years. For sweeteners, pioneers made do with honey or with syrup

From *Everyday Life: The Frontier* © 1999 Good Year Books.

obtained by boiling the sap from maple trees. A kind of coffee was made by boiling sassafras root or brewing parched corn and barley.

The standard cooking utensil was the iron pot. It was suspended over the fire on an iron arm called a lugpole. Most meals were of the one-pot variety prepared in the big pot, where they were sometimes kept warm for days. But pioneer women also made use of covered pans and spiders. A spider was a frying pan that sat on legs and had a long handle designed to keep its user from getting burned by the open fire. Covered pans also had legs and could be placed in hot coals or ashes to keep food warm. Meat cooked separately might be grilled on a four-legged iron rack.

Not all vegetables and fruits were eaten when gathered. Frontier women preserved vegetables by pickling and storing them in a cool place away from the fire. Fruits were turned into jellies and jams sweetened with honey or maple sugar. When finished, jellies and jams were poured into earthenware jars and sealed with a layer of mutton fat. Then the tops of the jars were covered with either greased paper or the bladder of an animal. (No kidding!) Meat was also saved for future use after being cured by smoking, salting, or drying.

As the frontier pushed across the Rocky Mountains, the foods eaten by pioneers changed somewhat. This was especially true in places where mining and cattle towns sprang up. With women scarce and men having to fend for themselves, flour, dried beans, and meat often made up the diet. Flour was used to make bread, sourdough biscuits, and flapjacks (pancakes). Bison, deer, elk, antelope, bacon, salt pork, beef, and jerky were standard meats. In short, miners and cowboys survived on a diet consisting primarily of meat and biscuits or flapjacks. They rarely ate fresh fruits or vegetables and apparently avoided dairy products at all costs because they seemed to think that fruits, vegetables, and milk were for tenderfoots and weaklings. Strong coffee, however, was an absolute necessity.

On long cattle drives from Texas northward, cowboys ate the same kinds of food, with beans (lots of them) added to the usual fare. Meals on cattle drives were served from chuck wagons. A chuck wagon was a rolling kitchen usually pulled by two teams of horses. It carried

A cowboy tells the story of Pecos Bill around the campfire after the evening meal. Storytelling was a major form of amusement on long cattle drives.

From Everyday Life: The Frontier © 1999 Good Year Books.

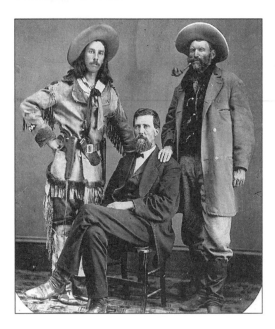

A mountain man (right) and an artist-scout (left) pose with a companion in this photograph taken about 1867. Such pictures accurately depict styles of clothing worn at the time.

enough food, bedding, and other items to last the long journey. It had a tailgate door which dropped down and formed a table for the cook to use while preparing meals. The cook was the chuck wagon's undisputed boss. He was usually paid $5 more a month than the cowboys, who earned an average of $30 a month. Any cowboy who insulted the cook or complained about his cooking might end up eating biscuits that were burned on the outside and raw in the middle.

Like food, clothing changed as the frontier shifted west. But in the early years, pioneers imitated the dress of the Indians. Trappers and hunters who first crossed the Appalachians in the 1700s set the standard for the settlers who followed later. They fashioned shirts, trousers, and moccasins out of deerskin and topped these off with raccoon or fox skin caps. Their hunting shirts were loose and open at the neck and often had fringed sleeves. Around their waists they wore a leather belt from which hung their bullet bag, tomahawk, and knife. In addition to hunters and trappers, it was not unusual to see an entire family of pioneers dressed in deerskin in the early days of the frontier.

To make deerskin softer, the hides were dried and soaked in hemlock or oak bark. Afterward, they were pounded and kneaded until they became flexible. Still, deerskin clothing was uncomfortable, and men usually wore an inner shirt and underwear made of linsey-woolsey. Women and children also wore clothing made of linsey-woolsey. Linsey-woolsey was a cloth made from combining linen and wool threads.

Pioneers usually did not have enough wool on hand, so they grew flax from which to make linen. The flax plant, when soaked, dried, and pounded, produced silky fibers that were hand-spun into linen thread on a small spinning wheel. The linen thread was then woven with those of wool to make linsey-woolsey. In time, men's clothing was also made from this homemade cloth. Linsey-woolsey was used to make clothing on the frontier from colonial times until well after the Civil War. After that, as the sewing machine slowly made its way west, other kinds of cloth were utilized. Those pioneers who were a part of the last frontier often wore "store bought" clothes if they could afford them.

From *Everyday Life: The Frontier* © 1999 Good Year Books.

Other pioneers who wore ready-to-wear clothes were forty-niners and cowboys. Prospectors, or forty-niners, caught up in the California Gold Rush of 1849 needed clothes in a hurry, and stores sprang up everywhere to supply them. Cowboys were not in that much of a hurry, but their rugged work demanded equally rugged clothes.

The most distinguishing feature of the cowboy on the western frontier was his headgear. A good felt hat made by the J. B. Stetson Company of Philadelphia sold for as much as $30. This, if you remember, was a full month's pay for most cowboys. But the hat was probably the most important part of the cowboy's attire. A good hat was designed to protect him from sun and rain, and its high crown served to keep his head cool. Because of its size, it could also be used as a water bucket. That is how it came to be called a "ten-gallon" hat.

Equally important to the cowboy were his boots. He often passed up $10 boots sold in stores in favor of a pair that were custom made. A good pair of boots might cost $25, but they were worth it to the cowboy. Besides satisfying the need for footwear, boots protected the wearer from such hazards as thorny bushes and poisonous snakes.

The cowboy attached spurs to the heels of his boots. These he used sparingly, only when it was necessary to urge his horse into action. Cowboy dandies (tenderfeet who wore fancy clothing) sometimes attached little metal ornaments called "jinglebobs" to their spurs, a practice which transformed them into walking wind chimes as they strode along!

The remainder of a cowboy's clothing included a wool shirt, a jacket or vest, and a bandanna that he wore around his neck for protection against dust and cold. He completed his attire with a pair of Levi trousers, over which he wore leather chaps to protect his legs from thorns and brushes. Although not a part of his apparel, a good saddle was a necessity. A cowboy sometimes paid twice as much for his saddle as he did for his horse.

While men wore typical cowboy clothing in cattle country, women generally dressed in sunbonnets and calico and gingham dresses. Calico is cotton cloth with colored patterns printed on one side. Gingham is cotton cloth made from colored thread. It is usually striped or checked.

Two miners dressed in Levis. Levis originated with Levi Strauss, a Jewish immigrant who began making the rugged trousers for California gold miners in the 1850s.

From Everyday Life: The Frontier © 1999 Good Year Books.

Name _____ Date _____

Flapjacks from the Chuck Wagon

Consumers today can go to the frozen foods section of their supermarket and buy such breakfast foods as pancakes and waffles already prepared. All they have to do is place the foods in their toaster or oven and they are ready to eat in only a few minutes.

Pioneers and cowboys, of course, did not enjoy such conveniences. All dishes had to be prepared from scratch and cooked over a fireplace or open fire. Except for the fact that you will be using a modern stove, you can cook a stack of pancakes or flapjacks similar to those turned out by the cook of a chuck wagon. Ask your parents or another adult to help you.

Here are the ingredients you will need:

2 cups of flour

¼ cup sugar

1 tablespoon salt

2 eggs

2 cups milk

⅓ cup shortening, cooking oil, or melted margarine

Steps

1. Beat eggs thoroughly in a large mixing bowl.

2. Mix in milk and the shortening, cooking oil, or melted margarine.

3. Add flour, sugar, and salt, and stir until batter is smooth.

4. Drop enough batter to make one pancake in a hot, greased frying pan or skillet.

5. Using a spatula, turned the pancake over when the top side becomes bubbly.

6. Fry to a golden brown on the other side.

Your mixture should make about a dozen and a half small pancakes.

From *Everyday Life: The Frontier* © 1999 Good Year Books.

Name _____ Date _____

Solve a Clothing Puzzle

Across

1. Raccoon or fox skin _____.

2. Cotton cloth with a print on one side.

5. Linsey-_____.

7. Cowboy trousers.

8. Kerchief worn by cowboys.

10. Found on the heels of cowboy boots.

11. Ten-_____ hat.

Down

1. Leather covering worn over Levi's.

3. Cowboy footwear.

4. A soft leather shoe.

6. Plant used to produce linen.

9. Early frontier clothing material.

From Everyday Life: The Frontier ©1999 Good Year Books.

Name _____ Date _____

Solve Some Cowboy Math Problems

Just in case you thought cowboys never had to worry about math, check out these three problems. Space is provided for you to work each problem, along with lines on which to write your answers.

1. Before heading west to seek his fortune, Hopalong Henry borrowed $125 from Shyster Skinflint to outfit himself as a proper cowboy. He agreed to repay the money, plus 20% interest, in eight equal installments. Therefore, Hopalong had to pay Mr. Skinflint $_____ each month. Since Hopalong only earned $30 a month, this meant that he had just $_____ left each time he made a payment.

2. Hopalong Henry paid $25 for his boots, $30 for his Stetson hat, and $20 for his horse. If he paid twice as much for a saddle as he paid for his horse, how much did he spend altogether? $ _____.

3. Chuck Wagon Charlie, the cook, must do some figuring. He knows that two cups of flour will make enough flapjacks to feed four hungry cowboys. If three and one-fourth cups are equal to one pound of flour, how many pounds will he need to feed a group of forty? _____ pounds (Round your answer.)

From *Everyday Life: The Frontier* ©1999 Good Year Books.

Name _____ Date _____

Find the Main Idea

Good paragraphs should contain one central, or main, idea. How good are you at picking these out?

Look back at the narrative and reread the paragraphs listed below. On the lines following each, write what you consider to be its main idea.

Paragraph 2 _____

_____

Paragraph 5 _____

_____

Paragraph 8 _____

_____

Paragraph 11 _____

_____

Paragraph 14 _____

_____

Paragraph 16 _____

_____

Go back and reread paragraph 6. On the lines provided, list the details that support or relate to its main idea.

_____

_____

_____

_____

_____

_____

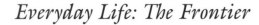

CHAPTER 4

Tasks and Chores

Every member of a frontier family had work to do. Only babies and toddlers were exempt, and even toddlers were assigned simple chores as early as possible. The youngest of children could feed chickens or gather sticks and twigs to help start fires. The combined work of an entire family was necessary to ensure survival in the wilderness.

Boys and girls on the frontier had many chores. One of the most important was keeping the family supplied with water. Until pioneers dug wells, children hauled water from the nearest spring or creek. Sometimes fathers made leather yokes with buckets hung from each end that fit over their youngsters' shoulders. Such yokes made carrying water easier and greatly reduced the number of trips back and forth to the spring. They also reduced the chance of spilling the water.

Water was a precious commodity on the frontier, and it was never wasted. Instead of dishwater simply being thrown out, it was used to water chickens and other livestock. Bathwater likewise saw secondhand use, as it was poured on flowers and plants. Little water, however, was actually used for bathing. Pioneers believed that bathing removed the skin's natural oils that protected them from illness. When they did bathe, they used the same large tub in which they washed their clothes. And since heating enough water to bathe in was quite a chore, the whole family often used the same bathwater!

A pioneer woman pushing a wheelbarrow loaded with buffalo or cow chips, the most common sources of fuel on the treeless plains.

Not only did boys and girls have to keep the house supplied with water, they also had to help their mothers and older sisters on wash day. Clothes were washed in a tub of hot water, with homemade lye soap used to remove the dirt. Young children often stood for hours pushing and poking at the clothes with sticks. Their action served the same purpose as agitators in modern washing machines. When the clothes were clean, they were hand-wrung and hung out to dry. On the plains, where trees were at a minimum, clothes were dried on the ground. In the winter they would freeze stiff, and during the frequent prairie windstorms, they might be ripped to shreds.

Another major chore of pioneer children was

From *Everyday Life: The Frontier* © 1999 Good Year Books.

collecting fuel for cooking and heating. In wooded areas, older children chopped, split, and stacked firewood. Younger children, as previously mentioned, gathered twigs and sticks. On the treeless plains, children gathered cow chips and buffalo chips. This dried animal dung, baked hard by the blazing sun, sometimes was the only source of fuel available.

Youngsters gathered chips in baskets and buckets and brought them home, where they were stored in old gunnysacks. Their mothers and older sisters, at first reluctant to pick up dried dung without gloves, eventually got so they could gather the chips with bare hands and toss them into a wheelbarrow or their aprons. There was no place for prudery or squeamishness on the American frontier.

Carrying water and collecting fuel were but two chores assigned to younger pioneer children. There were many more. Youngsters gathered eggs and hoed and weeded vegetable gardens. They milked cows and goats and herded hogs and sheep. They chased deer out of the fields and kept squirrels from eating the corn crop. They went on excursions to find wild nuts, berries, fruit, and herbs.

Boys and men cutting and raking grain in Wisconsin around the year 1875. The man second from the left is holding a scythe, a farm implement used for cutting grain and other grasses.

Older boys helped their fathers with the hardest tasks. They learned to plow and plant fields and to pitch hay. They helped their fathers build cabins and fences. They learned to hunt and trap animals and how to prepare skins for use as clothing and other purposes. Just as older daughters and their mothers sometimes had to help with the heavy farm work, boys and their fathers sometimes pitched in and helped with the cooking and washing, showing that a family worked together to make it on the frontier.

In cattle country, after the frontier had pushed farther west, boys (and sometimes girls) learned at an early age to handle and ride horses. It was not unusual for a lad of five or six to know how to sit in a saddle. By the time he was a teenager, that same boy could handle a team of horses pulling a wagon or plow. He was also old enough to set out on horseback to mend a fence or search for a lost calf.

Sometimes older boys were sent on missions that today would be viewed as extremely dangerous. A California schoolteacher wrote of a boy of fifteen

From *Everyday Life: The Frontier* © 1999 Good Year Books.

who attended school infrequently because he was always needed at home to work or to run errands. When not attending class, the boy was likely to be driving a wagon loaded with fruit and vegetables 150 miles over the Sierra Nevada mountains from California to Nevada. He stayed there just long enough to sell his produce to the miners before turning around to head home. He was completely alone and responsible for his own safety and well-being. On the way to and from his destination, he had to camp out at night and cook his own food. All the while, he had to feed and water his team of horses and make any necessary repairs to his wagon. If not-too-friendly Indians happened to be in the vicinity, he had to look out for them too. Quite a load for a young man of fifteen!

Older girls helped their mothers with household chores. They cooked, washed clothes, and helped clean the cabin or house. They sewed and knitted and spun flax, wool, or cotton into thread or yarn. They baked bread, churned butter, and helped with the canning and preserving. They made pillows, blankets, and coverlets. And if their family owned geese, they helped fill pillows and feather beds with goose feathers.

Performing household chores on the frontier. The girl in the middle and the woman at the right are churning butter.

Helping to make soap and candles were two other tasks of older girls. Soap was made once a year in the spring, and enough cakes were turned out to last throughout the year. Candles were usually made in the winter, when outdoor chores and activities were somewhat restricted because of the cold.

The first step in making soap was to put wood ashes saved during the winter into a large barrel. Then hot water was poured over the ashes. Slowly, the water filtered through the ashes and dripped through a hole in the bottom of the barrel, making lye. Next, the lye was boiled slowly in a large kettle with grease and animal fat until it thickened and formed a soft, yellow soap. If ammonia and borax were available, they could be added to part of the mixture to make laundry soap. To make a pleasant-smelling hand soap, bayberry might be used.

Before molds became available, candles were made by dipping wicks into melted tallow, or hard animal fat. Several dippings were required before the

From *Everyday Life: The Frontier* © 1999 Good Year Books.

candles reached the desired thickness. Between dips, the candles were allowed to cool. Sometimes several wicks were slipped over a candle rod and dipped into the kettle of hot tallow, making it possible to make more than one candle at a time. With molds, six or eight candles could be made in quick fashion. Melted tallow was simply poured into the molds and allowed to harden around homemade wicks inserted in the middle.

Making soap and candles were important tasks on the frontier. So too were the making of clothes and simple furniture, as you learned in Chapters 2 and 3. But pioneers, especially those who helped tame America's earlier frontiers, also made many of their own tools. Sometimes the only tool a pioneer family carried into the wilderness was an ax. Everything else had to be made by hand.

For the making of tools, frontier cabins doubled as workshops. At night, long after the outside chores were finished, men and boys used the light from the fireplace to make kitchen utensils, wooden rakes, flails, pitchforks, spades, plow blades, and even watering troughs. You can imagine the time and labor required to chisel a watering trough out of a large log.

Building fences was another necessary task on the frontier. Pioneers built fences to keep animals out, rather than in. Most early fences were of the rail type. Logs were split and laid in zigzag fashion to make up for the absence of nails. To seal off gardens, picket-style fences were erected. Fences served the purpose of protecting crops from larger animals such as hogs, but no kind of fence could keep some animals—such as squirrels—from having a go at young plant sprouts or ears of corn. That is why younger pioneer children kept a vigilant watch on the fields and gardens.

Life on the frontier was hard. Everyone worked from sunrise to sunset just to survive. Frontier living was especially hard on women. Childbearing took its toll, as did the day-to-day supervision of children. Besides taking care of a multitude of household chores, women sometimes had to help the men and boys with planting and plowing. As a result, many frontier women died young. That old saying from the *New England Primer,* "Man may work from sun to sun, but woman's work is never done," was never more true than during frontier days.

Sometimes townspeople got together to do a chore. This illustration depicts a Flax Scutching Bee. "To scutch" means to beat flax to remove the woody part.

From *Everyday Life: The Frontier* © 1999 Good Year Books.

Name _____ Date _____

Compare Frontier Chores with Yours

Most young people today have chores to do at home. Your personal chores may consist simply of keeping your room clean and perhaps taking out the garbage. Or your chores may be more numerous and detailed.

Under the column headings, list the chores you do at home, the chores pioneer children generally did, and the chores common to you both.

My Chores	Chores of Pioneer Children	Common Chores

Name _____ Date _____

Create a Dialogue

Pretend that a time machine has whisked you back to the Kentucky frontier of the late 1700s. You see Matthew and Sarah Harris performing a variety of chores: gathering fuel for the fireplace, carrying water from a stream to their cabin, and helping their parents make soap and candles—to name a few. As you smile and shake your head in disbelief, you begin telling them about the everyday conveniences of modern times.

On the lines provided, create a dialogue between Matthew, Sarah, and yourself in which you describe the wonders of the 20th century.

Name _____ Date _____

Make a Mobile

You have learned that children on the frontier had many chores. You can make a mobile depicting these chores with a few simple materials.

Here Is What You Will Need:

1. Clothes hanger (the larger the better)

2. Different-colored construction paper

3. String

4. Hole punch

5. Felt-tip pen

6. Some stiff wire

Here Is What You Do:

1. Make chore tags by cutting different colors of construction paper into small sizes (about 2 in. square). Leave some tags square, and cut the others into various shapes: rectangles, triangles, circles, stars, etc.

2. On each side of the tags, write the name of one chore assigned to pioneer children (chopping wood, carrying water, making candles, etc.).

3. Punch a hole at the top of each tag.

4. Insert and tie a piece of string through the hole at the top of each tag. Make your pieces of string different lengths so you can stagger the chore tags on the clothes hanger.

5. Attach the chore tags to the bottom of the clothes hanger.

6. Make a sign reading "Chores of Pioneer Children" and attach it to the top of the hanger.

To make a more detailed mobile, cut pieces of stiff wire in 6-in. lengths. Slightly bend each piece in the middle to give it a rainbow shape. Attach a chore tag to each end of the wire strips. Tie different lengths of string to the middle of each piece of wire and hang chore tags on each string. Attach the strings to the bottom of the clothes hanger.

From *Everyday Life: The Frontier* ©1999 Good Year Books.

Name _____ Date _____

Solve Some Chore-Related Math

Jacob and Esther Boone have seven children. Because it is wash day, each child is told to bring as many buckets of water as possible from the creek to the family cabin in the clearing. The results of their labor are shown in the chart.

Look back through your math book and review mean, mode, median, and range. You will need this information to solve the problems related to the chart.

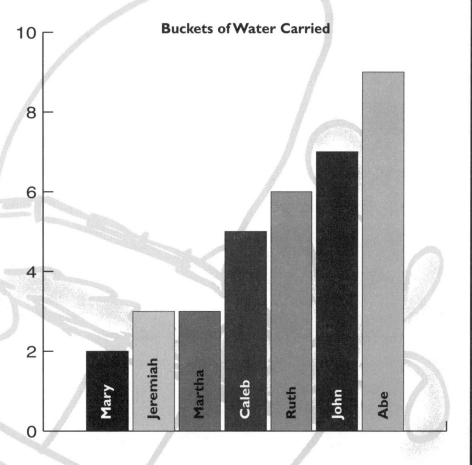

Buckets of Water Carried

1. Using the chart above, what number represents the mode? _____

   median? _____

2. What is the range? _____ the mean _____?

3. Using the chart, create a word problem of your own in the space below. Ask a classmate to solve it.

From *Everyday Life: The Frontier* © 1999 Good Year Books.

CHAPTER 5

Dangers and Hardships

Chapter 4 ended with a summary of how difficult life was on the frontier. It pointed out that pioneer women, because of the rigors of childbearing and hard work, often died young. But there were others on the frontier who suffered even more deeply than those brave pioneer women: their own children. A check of pioneer cemeteries throughout the West shows that the vast majority of graves are those of young children whose frail bodies could not withstand the hardships of frontier living.

Whether on the early or later frontier, a constant threat to life was sickness and disease. With few doctors available and only home remedies at hand, disease took a terrible toll. Typhoid, malaria, smallpox, cholera, yellow fever, and dysentery killed settlers and Native Americans alike. People also died from such illnesses as colds, influenza, and ear infections—diseases that cause only minor discomfort in today's world of modern medicine. Even when more doctors began to follow the pioneers west, they were too few in number and not always close by. Mothers lived in fear of having a child become seriously ill, knowing the nearest doctor was miles away and perhaps even across a river with no bridge to the other side.

Another concern of pioneers, especially those on the early frontier, was the threat of Indian attacks. This threat varied from area to

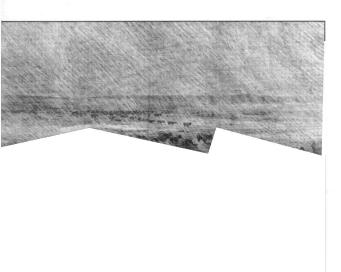

Cattle fall victim to a blizzard somewhere in Kansas. With no way to forecast extreme changes in the weather, sudden snowstorms took the lives of animals and humans alike.

area. In some places, settlers lived in almost constant fear of hostile Indians. In other places, the fear was less real. Just like the pioneers themselves, some Indians were friendly while others were not. Sometimes clashes sprang from acts committed by the Indians. Often as not, the trouble could be traced to some action on the part of the pioneers. All it took was an insult or a random killing by either side to spark a confrontation.

When settlers first came to the shores of North America in the seventeenth century, relations with the Native Americans were generally good. The Pilgrims in New England, in fact, would have starved without the help of Native Americans. They even served as guides for pioneers years later during the movement across the Great Plains to the Pacific Northwest. Tension

From *Everyday Life: The Frontier* © 1999 Good Year Books.

between the races only grew worse as Native Americans found more and more of their lands being taken from them. With their backs against the wall, the Native American had little choice but to resist the intrusion of the white man.

Although there were killings and kidnappings on the part of the Indians of the plains, such occurrences were rare after 1870. By that time, most of the plains tribes had been placed on reservations. Any Indian visit to a homestead most likely would be associated with hunger or curiosity. Sometimes several Indians would enter a house and sample what was cooking on the stove. At other times, the intruders might pick up and examine a baby lying in a cradle. Startled housewives learned to remain calm and give the Indians what they wanted. Often something to eat and perhaps an article or two of clothing was enough to make the uninvited guests vacate the premises.

Acts of nature posed a far greater threat to settlers than Native Americans. Pioneers on the plains had to contend with floods and tornadoes in the spring, drought and hailstorms in the summer, prairie fires in the fall, and blizzards and intense cold in the winter. Of these seasonal disasters, the most feared was fire.

A prairie fire usually stemmed from lightning or a campfire not properly attended. Once started, a prairie fire spread quickly from field to field. Driven by the wind, the flames raced along like a galloping horse, engulfing thousands and thousands of acres as it fed off the dry grass. Some fires lasted as long as six weeks before they could be brought under control. Wise pioneers who traveled on the Plains always carried matches with them in case they were trapped in one of these blazes. Many a traveler was spared a fiery death by burning out a circle of grassland to create a safe haven so the flames would pass harmlessly by.

When homesteaders saw the smoke of a fire approaching from a distance, they immediately set to work plowing a firebreak around their house. A firebreak was a furrow in which the grass in the rut was burned to prevent the fire from jumping across. A constant vigil was then necessary to stamp out

In this well-known lithograph by Currier and Ives, a train races across the prairie with a fire raging in the background. Prairie fires were the most feared of all the hazards associated with life on the Great Plains.

From Everyday Life: The Frontier © 1999 Good Year Books.

small fires that managed to spring up from sparks that blew across the furrow. Wet blankets and anything else at hand were used to prevent these small fires from escalating. There are even accounts of homesteaders killing a steer and dragging its bleeding body across the fire line to wet it.

Once the firebreak was completed and the threat to home and property diminished, a frontier family could take refuge inside their sod house. Soddies, especially when doused with water beforehand, afforded adequate protection against prairie fires. One pioneer woman was even known to increase her soddy's fireproof qualities by wetting it down with milk!

As fall passed and the threat of fire lessened, the people of the prairie braced for the next menace: winter, with its snowstorms and severe cold. Winter temperatures on the prairie were so cold that a person outdoors could freeze to death in a matter of minutes. Storms could be so fierce that in order to feed their livestock and perform other outside chores, pioneers sometimes strung a rope from the house to the barn so they would not lose their way in the blinding snow.

Children at a rural Kansas school race for an underground storm shelter as a tornado bears down on them. Tornadoes were but one of many dangers faced by settlers on the Plains.

Blizzards could strike suddenly and without warning. A terrible storm in 1888 was called the "schoolchildren's storm" because so many children were caught outside in it and died. All together, about 200 people were killed, most of them children on their way home from school. Among the victims were nine students and their teacher who were found frozen to death in a field not too far from their Dakota Territory schoolhouse. Untold numbers of cattle and other livestock also perished. Similar blizzards sometimes took the lives of entire families who were caught making a wagon trip to or from town. With weather forecasting in its infancy and communication unreliable, frontier folk had no way of knowing when a severe blizzard was heading their way.

The same was true of tornadoes. Today, thanks to state-of-the-art forecasting, people who live in areas prone to tornadoes can usually be given ample warning to prepare and take cover. But on the frontier, there was no way of predicting these terrible windstorms. Much destruction and loss of life

occurred as tornadoes, unimpeded by such natural barriers as mountains, raced across the plains.

Many pioneers who survived the ravages of winter and summer were finally defeated by another terror: locusts. From 1874 to 1878, huge armies of locusts plagued the plains. They suddenly appeared from east of the Rocky Mountains and destroyed everything in their path. In a matter of a few hours, a swarm of locusts could wipe out an entire wheat or corn crop. The destructive insects might appear at a homestead at four in the afternoon, and by sunset every stalk of every plant would be stripped bare. Efforts to halt their relentless march with fire failed. All frustrated settlers could do was stand by helplessly and watch their hopes and dreams destroyed.

Besides ravaging crops, locusts swarmed on people trying to stop their advance, and the pests literally had to be brushed from oneself. The locusts ate rope and anything made of hide. They fell into creeks and streams and ruined water supplies. They were so numerous that the ground was often covered to a depth of three or four inches with their swarming bodies. Sometimes the limbs of trees broke and fell under the weight of so many locusts.

But there was more. Pioneers, especially children, had to be on the lookout for poisonous snakes, ticks, spiders, flies, buffalo gnats, and ferocious wild pigs. Rabies was also a constant danger. In the years before the development of a vaccine for treatment, a large number of pioneers died after being bitten by rabid animals. Death from rabies was so horrible that stories exist of infected persons being left tied to trees to die away from their families.

With all the dangers present on the frontier, it is a wonder that anyone survived. Many didn't. Others gave up and went back East. But they were quickly replaced by newcomers who persevered and managed to tame the wilderness. On the Great Plains, where drought drove many homesteaders away, windmills appeared and provided water for the parched land. When barbed wire was invented and brought an end to the open range and its accompanying cattle drives, the great American frontier was conquered at last.

All that remains of a Kansas garden after a swarm of grasshoppers passed through. Grasshoppers could wipe out an entire crop in a matter of hours.

From Everyday Life: The Frontier © 1999 Good Year Books.

Name _____ Date _____

Finish a Frontier Story

In Chapter 5, you learned about the dangers associated with frontier life. Not the least of these dangers was tornadoes. With this in mind, complete a story that has been started for you. Lines are provided for you to expand on the story and give it any ending you desire.

Jordan and Allison were some distance from home gathering buffalo chips for the family fire. As they filled their baskets, their eyes were on dark storm clouds forming in the western sky.

"We'd better hurry," said Jordan. "Bad storm on the horizon there."

"Wow!" exclaimed Allison. "Look at those clouds rolling!"

They hurried their efforts to complete their chore. Suddenly, Allison pointed to the boiling sky.

"Look! A twister! A twister's coming!"

The two children abandoned their baskets and ran as fast as they could in the direction of their family's soddy. Coming over a hill, they spotted their father.

"Pa! Pa!" shouted Jordan. "A twister! There's a twister headed this way!"

_____

_____

_____

_____

_____

_____

_____

_____

_____

_____

_____

_____

Name _____ Date _____

Meet Mr. Locust! A Science-Related Activity

Do you know the difference between a grasshopper and a locust? Most people do not. Actually, a locust is a kind of grasshopper. It is different from the others in that it has shorter horns, or antennae. It was the locust that did millions of dollars in damage to crops in Kansas and Nebraska in the 1870s and 1880s.

Below is a sketch of a locust. Using an encyclopedia or a science book as a resource, label on the locust these external parts: antennae, compound eye, mouth, thorax, wing, foreleg, middle leg, and hind leg. Afterward, color your sketch.

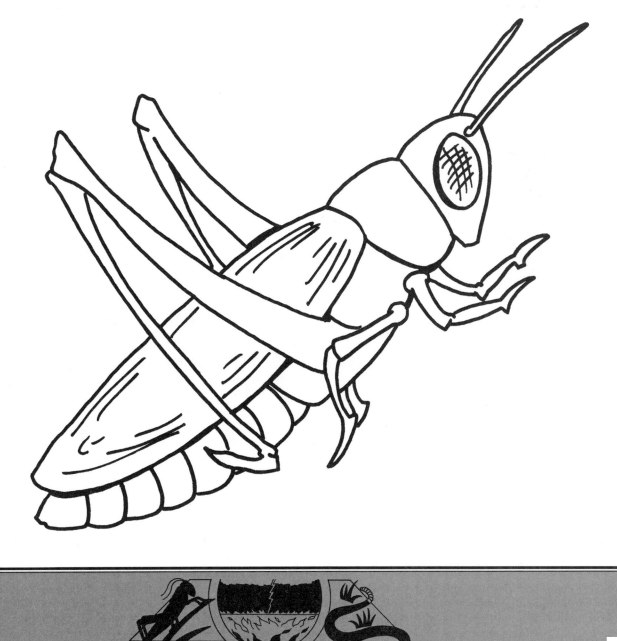

From Everyday Life: The Frontier ©1999 Good Year Books.

Name _____ Date _____

Complete a Vocabulary Exercise

Select the meaning of each word as it is used in Chapter 5. Write the letter of the correct meaning on the line at the left. The paragraph in which each word appears in the narrative is written in parentheses.

_____ 1. **minor** (paragraph 2)
(a) a person under the legal age of responsibility
(b) smaller
(c) a course of study requiring less time than a major

_____ 2. **spark** (paragraph 3)
(a) a small bit of fire
(b) a bright flash
(c) set off or stimulate

_____ 3. **attended** (paragraph 7)
(a) act of securing a seat or room in advance
(b) cared for or looked after
(c) served

_____ 4. **perform** (paragraph 10)
(a) do
(b) go through
(c) act, play, or sing in public

_____ 5. **field** (paragraph 11)
(a) stop or catch a batted ball
(b) open land
(c) area where contests are held

_____ 6. **stalk** (paragraph 13)
(a) the main stem of a plant
(b) walk stiffly and proudly
(c) pursue without being seen or heard

_____ 7. **present** (paragraph 16)
(a) a gift
(b) at hand
(c) offer

_____ 8. **range** (paragraph 16)
(a) place to practice shooting
(b) extent
(c) land for grazing

From *Everyday Life: The Frontier* © 1999 Good Year Books.

Name _____ Date _____

Use Your Critical Thinking Skills

Using the lines provided, write your best answers to the questions.

1. In your opinion, were whites or Native Americans more responsible for the bloodshed that sometimes occurred on the frontier? Were they equally responsible? Give facts to support your answer.

_____
_____
_____
_____
_____

2. Which danger associated with frontier living do you think posed the greatest threat to pioneers? Why?

_____
_____
_____

3. What personal traits would better enable a pioneer to withstand the hardships of frontier life?

_____
_____
_____

4. How might history have turned out differently if pioneers had given up hope of settling the Great Plains?

_____
_____
_____
_____

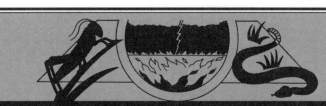

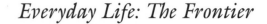

CHAPTER 6

Frontier Schools

In the early years of the frontier, schools were almost nonexistent. What learning children acquired came from their parents. But as the frontier spread farther west, first across the Rocky Mountains and then onto the Great Plains, pioneers began to recognize the need to provide a more formal education for their children. So they built rough schoolhouses before they built their own dwellings.

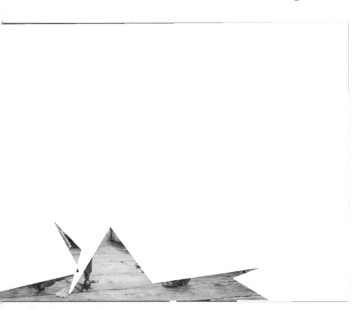

Students recite for their teacher in a typical one-room frontier schoolhouse. From a painting by E. L. Henry.

Typical frontier schoolhouses were one-room structures built either of logs or sod. They were dark, poorly equipped, and highly uncomfortable. On the early frontier, students usually sat on three-legged stools and worked at desks that were nothing more than shelves fastened to the wall. In some places, seats consisted of two boards balanced on rocks. Later, wooden benches and then regular desks were introduced. For heat, students huddled around a cast-iron stove, usually situated in the middle of the room. (The "potbellied" stove remained a feature of country schools for at least a half century after the frontier ended. Many people, the author included, have fond memories of constantly feeding coal to the big stove on cold winter days and watching it glow red hot. Small wonder that only a few of these small country schools ever went up in smoke!)

Early schools had no chalkboards and few books. A painted piece of wood often took the place of a blackboard, and children brought what books they had at home with them to class. Many had only the Bible and perhaps an old almanac. Others had these, plus maybe a dictionary, an encyclopedia, or a history book. Still others might have had *McGuffey's Reader* and *Webster's Speller*. Often these books brought from home were the only supplies in the room. In the early days of the frontier, there were no maps or globes available, and students did not even have slates until about 1825. Lead pencils appeared much later than that.

Emphasis in frontier schools was on the three Rs: reading, 'riting, and 'rithmetic. Sometimes there were also lessons in geography and history.

From *Everyday Life: The Frontier* © 1999 Good Year Books.

Because students in the one-room school might range in age from toddlers to late teens, they were not separated into grade levels. The teacher worked with one or two students at a time while the others studied or did lessons. Sometimes the older students helped the younger ones. Lessons involved much memory work, and students read and recited passages in front of the class. Both reading and spelling were practiced aloud. Time was also set aside to practice penmanship and compete in spelling bees.

Whereas students today have certain classroom tasks they are asked to perform (washing the chalkboard, etc.), frontier children had outright chores. Since everyone drank from the same pail and dipper, students took turns filling the pail from the school well. If they expected a fire to heat the building, they had to provide the fuel. In forested areas, boys and girls chopped and gathered wood. On the plains, they went out with baskets and brought back buffalo or cow chips.

At recess, students played games still popular today. Marbles were a favorite with the boys, as were jacks and jump rope with the girls. Younger students enjoyed playing hide-and-seek and drop the handkerchief. Sometimes older boys played horseshoes or mumblety-peg, a game in which they flipped a pocketknife and tried to make it stick firmly in the ground or some wooden object. Recess was probably all the more enjoyable because of the dogs that followed their owners to school. While the students were in class, the dogs lay outside the schoolhouse door, whining. Sometimes they would sneak in and lie at their owner's feet.

Getting to school in frontier times was an adventure. Most students walked, but others came on horseback or in wagons. One picture taken in the late 19th century shows seven young boys making the journey on the back of one very patient cow. In time, school "buses" in the form of horsedrawn carriages appeared in some areas.

Frontier children got to school any way they could. These seven boys hitched a ride on the back of a cow.

The length of school terms on the frontier varied. Sometimes they were no longer than three months. Chores at home, especially during times of plowing and planting, came first. Some youngsters never attended school at all, and many did not begin their first day until well into their teens.

Since school terms were often short, teachers had to find other means of

From Everyday Life: The Frontier © 1999 Good Year Books.

livelihood during the months classes were not in session. Their pay of $10 to $35 a month applied only to the months school was open. To offset such low income, teachers boarded, or lived, with their students' families. They might stay one week with one family and one week with another until they had completed the circuit.

Who were these brave souls who ventured west to teach the children of the pioneers? At first, some were no more than children themselves—fifteen and sixteen years old. No formal training was required to teach, and anyone with an elementary knowledge of reading and math might be hired. In reality, the absence of any uniform requirements for becoming a teacher continued in some places well into the 1900s.

Students at a later frontier school play Ring-Around-the-Rosie. Other games included jump rope and hide-and-seek, still favorites with school children today.

One gentleman in California who had failed as a gold prospector thought he would try his hand at teaching. When he came before the school trustees (one of whom was a saloon keeper) to apply for a position, he was quite apprehensive about his chances of getting the job. On the table where the three trustees sat was a spelling book. One opened the speller and gave the prospective teacher his "comprehensive" examination. The applicant was asked to spell *cat, hat, mat,* and *rat.* When he successfully did, he was hired on the spot. In time, qualified teachers from the East made their way to the frontier, and the level of instruction in the one-room schoolhouses improved considerably.

Discipline was sometimes a problem in frontier schools. This was especially true when the teacher was a young man not much older than some of his students. Husky boys who had driven wagons across mountains and prairie and who might have fought hostile Indians along the way often gave male teachers a rough time. Many of these older boys spit chewing tobacco all over the room and whistled and made loud noises to disrupt lessons. They pestered the girls and picked on the younger students. If and when they ever took a seat, a fistfight usually broke out.

To maintain a semblance of order, frustrated men teachers had to rely on the switch and even the rawhide whip. One reported that he had whipped thirteen delinquent boys on the very first day of school! He continued to flog troublemakers each day until his discipline problems subsided.

From *Everyday Life: The Frontier* © 1999 Good Year Books.

Another young male teacher in California headed off any discipline problems in a unique way. Sensing he had inherited a particularly rough group of teenage boys, he stood before the class on opening day, drew his six-shooter from its holster, and placed it on his desk. He then announced that if anyone misbehaved, there was going to be trouble. One can only assume that this young teacher's "six-shooter discipline" was highly effective.

Women teachers usually fared better with students. For the most part, they were respected because they were women. They also benefited from the fact that no one expected them to engage in physical combat with disrespectful teenagers. A stern look on their part was often enough to control the most obnoxious farm boy, who knew he might be whipped at home when his parents learned that he had given the "schoolmarm" a hard time.

Much credit is due these brave women who left comfortable homes in the East and traveled alone to teach on the frontier. They were often homesick and lonely, and their opportunities for leisure activities were limited and usually restricted. In many places, they were even forbidden to marry.

Besides fulfilling the educational needs of children, frontier schools sometimes doubled as community centers and churches. They were often the site of the Saturday night dances that were such an important part of community entertainment on the frontier. For a few hours, weary pioneers could forget the cares of the day and relax and enjoy themselves.

Children also enjoyed community dances, and not always for the purest of reasons. The dances provided a rare opportunity for mischief that some of the bolder students took advantage of. A favorite prank while a dance was in progress was to switch babies asleep in their baskets. Mothers left their babies in baskets near the schoolhouse door or just off the dance floor, and, when no one was looking, children sometimes switched the babies from basket to basket. Often the sleepy parents were well on their way home before they discovered the baby in their basket was not theirs. There followed a hurried retreat back to the schoolhouse, where confused parents sorted our the babies and tried to determine which rascally children's ears to box!

Students and their teacher pose in front of their sod schoolhouse in Nebraska around 1900. All grades were taught together, which accounts for the wide age differences among students.

Name _____ Date _____

Compare Frontier Schools with Yours

On the lines below the headings "Frontier Schools" and "Your School," write pertinent facts about each.

	Frontier Schools	**Your School**
1. Building size	_____	_____
2. Students' ages	_____	_____
3. Attendance	_____	_____
4. Textbooks used	_____	_____
	_____	_____
5. Available supplies	_____	_____
	_____	_____
6. Teacher qualifications	_____	_____
	_____	_____
7. Getting to school	_____	_____
	_____	_____
8. Discipline	_____	_____
	_____	_____
9. Length of school term	_____	_____
	_____	_____
10. Subjects studied	_____	_____
	_____	_____
11. Heating	_____	_____
	_____	_____
12. Classroom chores or responsibilities	_____	_____
	_____	_____

From *Everyday Life: The Frontier* © 1999 Good Year Books.

Name _____ Date _____

Write a Letter About a Frontier School

Pretend you are a schoolteacher and that you have just completed your first day of teaching in a frontier school. Write a letter to a friend back East describing your experiences and first impressions. You decide whether your first day was exhilarating or if it was something you would just as soon forget.

Date _____

Dear _____

_____

_____

_____

_____

_____

_____

_____

_____

_____

_____

_____

_____

_____

_____

_____

_____

Sincerely,

_____

Name _____ Date _____

Interpret a Bar Graph

Most frontier communities eventually built some kind of school to meet their children's educational needs. Some schools had only a handful of students; others might have as many as thirty (a large number for those days). Schools were usually constructed so that boys and girls would not have to walk more than two or three miles to reach the classroom. Thus, a district, or a region in a state or territory, would have a number of schools.

The bar graph indicates how many children attended each school in a mythical district. Using the information indicated on the graph, answer the questions.

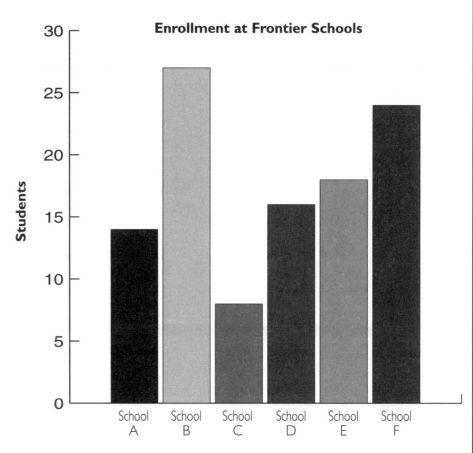

1. How many students attended school in the district altogether? _____

2. What percentage of the district's students attended School B? _____%

3. What percentage attended School C? _____%

4. What was the average number of students at each school? _____ (round to the nearest one)

5. What is the range, or the difference, between the highest and lowest number of students? _____

6. Is a mode represented among the numbers? (Yes, No)

Name _____ Date _____

Use Your Critical Thinking Skills

Read each of the situations. Then draw your own conclusions to answer the questions. Write your answers on the lines provided.

1. Young Mary Perkins has a knack for art. She is especially talented at drawing sketches of people. But because of the limited curriculum and the number of students attending her frontier school, her teacher has neither the time nor the inclination to encourage Mary's artistic ability.

What will probably happen to Mary's interest in art, and why?

_____

_____

2. Two husky farm boys are taunting a new teacher in a frontier school. The teacher, a young man of small stature fresh from the East, is at a loss as to what he should do. After a while, two smaller boys turn to the bullies and tell them to shut up and sit down.

What can you conclude might have happened next?

_____

_____

3. Joshua Lawrence's father informs him that the horse he has ridden three miles to school every day for several years is now needed for work on the farm. He assures Joshua that school is not all that important anyhow. Mrs. Lawrence disagrees but maintains that three miles is much too far for a boy of Joshua's age to walk to school.

How do you think Joshua's future education will be affected?

_____

_____

4. Ms. Clay, a teacher in School A, has only 10 students in her charge. Mr. White, on the other hand, is responsible for 33 students in his one-room schoolhouse.

Why do the students in Ms. Clay's school have a decided advantage?

_____

_____

_____

CHAPTER 7

Fun and Amusements

Life on the frontier was not all work. There was time for entertainment, and quite often work itself was turned into a form of play. House-raisings and barn-raisings, along with various kinds of bees, provided amusement for people throughout the frontier period.

Friends who gathered on a neighbor's plot of land could raise an entire house or barn in a day. Work began at sunup and continued until sundown.

While men and boys concerned themselves with carpentry tasks, women and girls put together a sumptuous feast to be eaten after the house or barn was finished. Often a lively square dance concluded the day's activities.

Bees afforded frontier people the opportunity for friendly competition in various kinds of work. In addition to quilting bees and husking bees, there were bees for removing stones and for cutting down trees. Even when there was no bee, frontier people enjoyed getting together for wrestling, foot races, and weight-lifting contests. Competition was keen, and it helped to mold the character of at least one famous American. A frontiersman in Indiana who could out-run, out-wrestle, and out-lift any boy or man around went on to become the 16th President of the United States. His name was Abraham Lincoln.

Weddings provided frontier people with yet another form of entertainment. Frontier weddings were riotous affairs, as every attempt was made to embarrass the happy couple. Often trees and other obstacles were placed across paths to delay the wedding party's arrival at the site of the ceremony. Spoilsports not invited to a particular wedding entertained themselves by playing pranks on those who were. Sometimes this involved cutting the tails and manes off the horses of the people in attendance.

Boys and girls of the early frontier often lived in such isolation that they had few if any playmates. But social gatherings like bees and house-raisings gave them the opportunity to play the same games as children back East—games with which you are familiar. Tag, hopscotch, and hide-and-seek were among their favorites. Any toys they enjoyed were homemade. Tops were

An English wax-head doll dating to 1885. Many little girls on the frontier, however, had to be satisfied with dolls made from corn husks.

carved from wood and marbles were fashioned from clay. Little girls played with dolls made from cornhusks. Children, as well as adults, played checkers on a board made of wood and with checkers cut from corncobs.

As the frontier pushed farther west, play and amusement varied from area to area. Both children and adults on the prairie enjoyed the same bees and house-raisings and barn-raisings as earlier pioneers. Children also delighted in the wide-open spaces of the prairie. They combined picnics with berry picking and collecting cow chips for fires. They amused themselves by seeing who could throw a cow chip the farthest. When a chip hit the ground and exploded, as it often did, everyone laughed—except, of course, those who happened to be standing near the point of impact!

Some frontier folk lived near towns, where exciting things were always happening. For a few pennies, youngsters and adults alike could thrill to the acts of jugglers, sword swallowers, and snake charmers. Just as entertaining to watch were the patent medicine peddlers. In booming voices, they hawked such miraculous cure-alls as Hamlin's Wizard Oil and Dr. John Bull's Vegetable Worm Destroyer. The peddlers often used magicians and other acts to attract gullible buyers to their stands or wagons.

Most towns had theaters where both amateurs and professionals acted out everything from slapstick comedies to Shakespearean plays. Boisterous audiences got their money's worth by yelling encouragement and suggestions to the actors. Sometimes, when not pleased with the performance they were watching, a rowdy audience might throw objects at bewildered entertainers on stage.

Traveling circuses moved through the West and stopped for shows at each town. A circus coming to town was an exciting event for frontier youngsters. Long before the circus reached the site where it was to be set up, boys and girls sprinted out to meet it. They ran alongside the wagons, marveling at the elephants and the wild animals snarling in their cages. And they surely stared in awe at the sight of the hippopotamus cage that required fourteen horses to pull it.

Some frontier families were better off than others. Besides the piano and modern pot-bellied stove, note the wallpaper and ornate picture frames.

From *Everyday Life: The Frontier* © 1999 Good Year Books.

Once the circus reached its destination, some youngsters volunteered to help put up the big tent and unload and feed the animals. The circus coming to town was without doubt the most exhilarating occurrence for the people of the frontier. In the 1870s, when circuses began traveling by rail, performances became even better. In addition to all the wonderful acts and wild animals, famous opera stars such as Jenny Lind and actresses such as Sarah Bernhardt performed in front of frontier audiences. Small wonder that the circus came to be called "The Greatest Show on Earth."

Frontier towns also gave people the opportunity to have their pictures taken. Although photography was still in its infancy, traveling photographers were commonplace in the West by the 1850s. Cameras were crude and cumbersome, and taking and developing a picture took a long time. But frontier people did not mind the wait. For many, a photograph taken in town was the only picture made of them in their lifetimes.

A German May Day parade in Weaverville, California, in 1860. May Day, along with Christmas and the Fourth of July, were favorite holidays among frontier folk.

As the frontier spread ever westward from 1770 on and each area was made a part of the United States, one holiday in particular took on special meaning for the hardy pioneer folk. That holiday was the Fourth of July. It was such a special occasion that everyone who could came to town early for a day filled with fun and laughter.

A resounding boom from either the town's cannon or from gunpowder exploded on a blacksmith's anvil told homesteaders for miles around that the day's activities were soon to begin. Families quickly finished their morning chores and loaded into wagons decorated with small flags and colored bunting. In high spirits, they headed for town and the most exciting day of the year.

Most Fourth of July celebrations began with patriotic speeches by the town leaders. This was followed by a parade led by a band and the local militia. When midday arrived, families gathered together and ate what they had brought in their picnic baskets. Afterward, they all looked forward to an afternoon filled with games and contests.

From *Everyday Life: The Frontier* © 1999 Good Year Books.

Every imaginable kind of competition characterized the Fourth. There were sack races and foot races for the boys and girls, and horse races and wagon races for the men. There were ball games, shooting matches, and pie-eating contests. If boys and men had any energy left after all the games, they might compete to see who could climb a greased pole or catch and hold a greased pig.

As the afternoon wore on, women produced skillets they had brought from home and cooked a huge meal that might include fried catfish and corn dodgers (fried cornbread). Then, as evening ebbed and darkness approached, a fireworks display dazzled all those present. The fireworks were undoubtedly the highlight of the day for the children. The highlight of the day for the young men and women was the dance, which began after the fireworks ended and sometimes continued until midday on July 5.

Young and old alike enjoy a taffy-pull party at Christmastime. As with various bees, refreshments and a dance always followed the completion of the task.

Another holiday important to frontier people was Christmas. But Christmas in those days was celebrated more simply than it is today. There were no Christmas cards, and few people purchased gifts. Children received toys that were homemade, such as cornhusk dolls and carved wooden tops. If a family was lucky, they might live near a forested area where they could cut and drag home an evergreen tree to be decorated.

Do you know any family today that still enjoys decorating a tree with old-fashioned paper chains and strings of popcorn or cranberries? On the frontier, such homemade decorations were the only kind at hand. Electric lights, tinsel, and glass ornaments were still years away. But frontier folk made do with what they had. In addition to making colored-paper chains and strands of popcorn and cranberries, they made candle holders out of tin and attached them to the branches of the tree. Sometimes they made a star for the top out of wire and paper.

Do you think you would have enjoyed the holidays and amusements that were so important to the people of the frontier?

Name _____ Date _____

Fill in a Venn Diagram

Fill in the Venn diagram to compare a frontier Fourth of July with the Fourth as it is celebrated in your home town. Write facts about each in the appropriate place. List features common to both where the circles overlap.

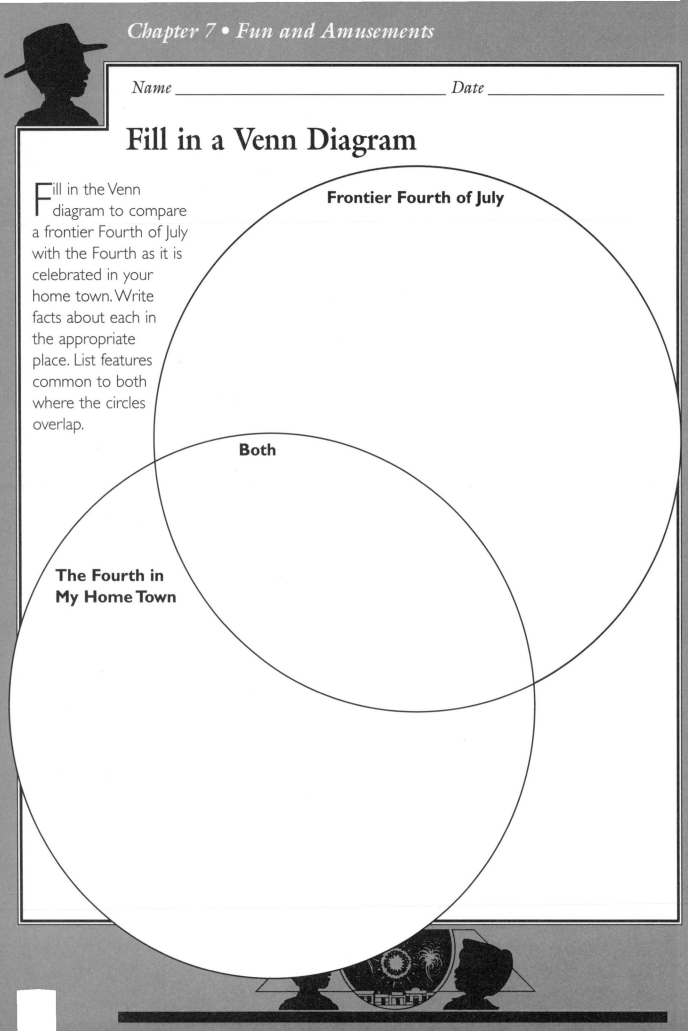

Frontier Fourth of July

Both

The Fourth in My Home Town

From Everyday Life: The Frontier © 1999 Good Year Books.

Name _____ Date _____

Write a Lead Paragraph for *Frontier Frolics*

Years passed before newspapers reached the people of the frontier. But, for the sake of this activity, imagine that a newspaper called *Frontier Frolics* already existed on the Kentucky frontier in the year 1792. Also imagine that you are one of the newspaper's roving reporters.

Write the lead, or first, paragraph of a story about a cabin-raising that would go along with the headline. Be sure to include answers to the five "W" questions ("Who?" "What?" "When?" "Where?" and "Why?") that are characteristic of a good lead paragraph.

Frontier Frolics
★ ★ ★ ★ ★ April 8, 1792 ★ ★ ★ ★ ★

Guthrie Cabin Raised in Record Time
Good Time Had by All

_____

_____

_____

_____

_____

_____

_____

_____

_____

_____

_____

_____

_____

_____

_____

_____

_____

_____

_____

From *Everyday Life: The Frontier* © 1999 Good Year Books.

Name _____ Date _____

Make Frontier Holiday Decorations

You have learned that frontier people made their own Christmas tree decorations. You can get a feel for old-fashioned ornaments by making paper chains, strings of popcorn, or paper cutouts to use as decorations for any holiday you choose. Perhaps you and your family have done this in the past.

To Make Paper Chains You Will Need:

1. Several packages of colored construction paper

2. Paste, glue, or transparent tape

3. Scissors

4 A ruler

Cut strips of standard-sized construction paper into 1" × 6" sizes. (If you measure correctly, you should be able to get 18 strips from each sheet of paper.) Using paste, glue, or transparent tape, make interlocking chain links of the strips, connecting them as you proceed. You can alternate the colors as you work on one chain. The length of your finished product depends on the size of what you are decorating and on your patience.

To Make Strings of Popcorn You Will Need:

1. Several 3-oz bags of microwaveable popcorn (fat-free preferred)

2. A sewing needle

3. A spool of white thread

After threading the needle, simply slide the popcorn onto the thread piece by piece. You might find it cumbersome to work with one long piece of thread, so string the popcorn in 3' or 4' foot strands and then tie them together.

To Make Paper Cutouts You Will Need:

1. Any kind of paper (construction, computer, typing, etc.)

2. Colored pens or crayons

3. Scissors

4. Your imagination, or various cookie cutters to use as patterns

Trace design on paper and then cut out. Use colored pens or crayons to add details.

From *Everyday Life: The Frontier* © 1999 Good Year Books.

Name _____ Date _____

Solve Some Square Dance Word Problems

Square dances were popular forms of entertainment on the frontier. Although they were sometimes associated with such events as weddings, house-raisings, and holiday celebrations, they were also held as separate activities—often on a Saturday night. A barn, a schoolhouse, or an outdoor platform might provide the setting for an evening of fun.

Getting to the dance was not an easy task, especially in the early days of the frontier. People might have to walk or ride a horse many miles to reach the site. With this in mind, answer these word problems.

1. John lived 5 miles from Rogersborough, the site of the square dance. He had no transportation at his disposal other than his feet. If he walked quickly, he could cover 1 mile in 15 minutes. How long would it take John to arrive at the dance?

    _____ hr(s) and _____ minutes

2. Luke lived one-third the distance to Rogersborough as John. How much time would he need to reach the dance if he walked at the same pace?

    _____ hr(s) and _____ minutes

3. Jacob and Mary Reston lived some distance from the barn dance being held in Jackson Junction. They left their sod house by wagon at 3:00 P.M. and arrived at the dance at 6:30 P.M. The dance lasted until midnight. They spent the night with friends in Jackson Junction and arrived home the next morning at 11:30 A.M. How many hours were they gone from home?

    _____ hrs and _____ minutes

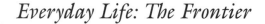

CHAPTER 8

Frontier Justice

For many years there was no established law or law enforcement on the frontier. There were few courts or law officers even in the latter days of the frontier period. As a result, pioneers often took matters into their own hands.

On the early Appalachian frontier, sometimes a tongue-lashing from neighbors was enough to straighten out a troublemaker. If that failed, a good flogging with a whip or hickory rod might work. Private arguments were often settled with the fists—or worse. Quarreling pioneers were not reluctant to go at each other with guns, knives, axes, or pitchforks. Often such clashes proved fatal to one or both of the parties.

When the frontier shifted to the Mississippi River, dueling became an accepted way of settling differences. One pioneer challenged another, and a location was established for the fight. Generally, the duel took place in the morning. The person challenged got to choose weapons, which were almost always pistols. Standing back to back, the duelers agreed to march a certain number of steps and wait for a signal from one of the "seconds" (friends who accompanied the quarrelers to the field of battle). At the drop of a handkerchief or some other signal, the adversaries turned and fired.

While tongue-lashings, floggings, and duels solved many problems on the frontier, another type of justice awaited horse thieves: lynching. A pioneer's most valued property was his horse, and to steal a horse was considered the worst crime possible. Horse thieves were hanged as soon as a suitable tree could be located, and usually without benefit of a trial.

Pioneers everywhere had unwritten laws of "fair play" which, surprisingly, most of them consented to and observed. A stray horse, for example, became the property of anyone who could catch and rope it. Another unwritten rule had to do with gunplay. As the frontier shifted ever westward, every man wore

In the absence of law and order on much of the frontier, pioneers such as these California gold miners usually took care of troublemakers and lawbreakers themselves.

From *Everyday Life: The Frontier* © 1999 Good Year Books.

a six-shooter to protect his life and property. But a code grew up governing shoot-outs. It was considered cowardly to shoot an unarmed man and even worse to shoot someone in the back. To bushwhack (ambush) a person was despicable. Amazing as it sounds, even desperadoes and outlaws for the most part recognized and followed this code.

A new method of dealing with lawbreakers developed in mining camps and spread to other parts of the frontier. This was the vigilante committee. The word *vigilante* comes from a Latin verb meaning "to watch." Vigilantes did more than simply watch; they took action, and it was often swift.

Although unauthorized and having no legal status, vigilante committees fulfilled a need in the absence of law and order. Even when areas of the West came under the jurisdiction of a U.S. Marshal, the marshal's territory was so large that he could not possibly settle every quarrel that arose or apprehend every person who broke the law. When he did arrest a lawbreaker, he often had no jail to hold him in. Vigilantes filled this void in law enforcement and carried out justice when necessary. Sometimes in their zeal they hanged an innocent person, but frontier people agreed that thugs hanged by the vigilantes got what they deserved.

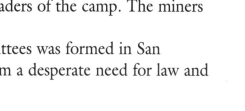

Frontier towns like Guthrie, Oklahoma, sprang up so quickly that no one gave much thought to law enforcement. Here a lawyer and a realtor carry on business even before setting up a tent.

Nowhere were vigilante committees more active than in California. The gold rush of 1849 brought every type of criminal across the Rockies to prey on law-abiding and defenseless miners. Lawbreakers jumped claims and robbed and killed with abandon. Some were so brazen that they stole mining equipment and sold it to newly arrived prospectors.

At first, miners attempted to control the criminal element through the use of the whipping post. They also tried tarring and feathering undesirables and banishing them from camp. When crime and violence increased, miners began to hang thieves and murderers. They established miner's courts presided over by one of the more respected leaders of the camp. The miners themselves made up the jury.

One of the better-known vigilante committees was formed in San Francisco in 1851. Its organization sprang from a desperate need for law and

order. For several years after gold was discovered, outlaws virtually ran the city, even though a police force had been formed in 1849. Two years later, a vigilante committee was organized. It hanged a number of thieves and murderers, often breaking into the city jail and dragging them away. The committee justified its action on the basis that the city was run by corrupt officials controlled by the criminal population. When honest officials were elected in 1855, the San Francisco Vigilante Committee disbanded and passed into history. That they were honored with a parade proved that people on the frontier welcomed any group that could maintain law and order, even if that group had no legal basis.

Vigilante committees sprang up in other territories and administered the same swift justice. When communities and towns became more orderly, such groups gave way to judges and courts. A number of colorful judges then appeared to write their names in the history of the West. One of the most famous was Judge Roy Bean of Langtry, Texas.

Judge Roy Bean's court house at Langtry, Texas. The judge doubled as a notary public, performed weddings, and, as one sign indicates, served up alcoholic beverages.

Langtry was a small town populated primarily by workers laying track for the Southern Pacific Railroad. As a typical frontier community, it was rough and disorderly and in dire need of law and order. Roy Bean came on the scene in 1882 and filled that need, even though sometimes in comic fashion.

Bean was a drifter of questionable character who managed to get himself appointed justice of the peace in Langtry. He set up court in a shack that doubled as a courtroom and saloon. When the business-minded judge was not serving out justice, he was serving out drinks to customers. A large sign nailed to the porch of the shack proclaimed the judge to be the "Law West of the Pecos." Other signs read "Justice of the Peace" and "Judge Roy Bean, Notary Public." Besides giving rustlers and other badmen their just do, the judge presided over inquests and weddings. He always ended his marriage ceremonies with the statement: "May God have mercy on your souls." Ever looking to fill his pockets with a dollar, Judge Bean once fined a dead man

From *Everyday Life: The Frontier* © 1999 Good Year Books.

$40 for illegally carrying a weapon. The dead man, of course, had exactly that amount on his person.

Another judge who helped bring law and order to the western frontier was Isaac C. Parker. He was actually sent to Fort Smith, Arkansas, in 1875 by President Grant. The President asked Parker to stay a year and straighten things out. He accomplished this and more. He sentenced so many outlaws to the gallows that he soon became known as "The Hanging Judge."

Judge Parker's district ran all the way from western Arkansas to the Colorado line, taking in all of what is now Oklahoma. During his twenty-one years on the bench, he tried over 10,000 cases. These ranged from tax evasion and brawling to murder and rustling. He sentenced 168 men and 4 women to the gallows, but only 88—all men—were actually hanged. The others either had their sentences reduced by the White House or completely overturned by courts of appeal.

Wyatt Earp—a tough marshal who helped tame the West.

Judge Parker's hangings were public spectacles. Sometimes as many as six lawbreakers were strung up at one time. People came from miles around to watch, bringing with them even their youngest children. Besides ridding the countryside of a number of notorious criminals, the judge's hangings served as a bizarre form of entertainment for bored frontier folk.

Parker's public hangings came to an end in 1891. The federal government had had enough of his public shows and ordered that future hangings be carried out in private. Five years later, Parker's judgeship was taken away, and an era in frontier justice came to an end. Like Roy Bean in Texas, "The Hanging Judge" faded into history at about the same time the frontier was coming to an end.

James B. (Wild Bill) Hickok—a marshal, scout, marksman, and fearless police officer.

Sandwiched in between vigilante committees and hanging-minded judges were a number of respectable lawmen. Most of these can be seen portrayed in old cowboy movies. They tamed some of the toughest cow towns in the West and helped make the frontier a safer place in which to live. Included were Bat Masterson, Wyatt Earp, and "Wild Bill" Hickok. They were usually as tough as the badmen they were hired to control. Tom Smith, the one-time marshal of Abilene, Kansas, was famous for knocking out armed desperadoes with his bare fists. Through the efforts of such fearless men, law and order eventually came to the Wild West.

From Everyday Life: The Frontier © 1999 Good Year Books.

Name _____ Date _____

Distinguish Between Fact and Opinion

Can you tell the difference between a fact and an opinion? Sometimes it is not easy to do. In our daily conversations, we make statements we think are facts but which in reality are opinions. Facts are things that are true and can be proven; opinions are simply strong beliefs

Carefully read the dialogue between Jenna and Brian concerning law and order on the frontier. Then on the blank line to the left of each statement, write "F" if you think the statement is a fact. Write "O" if you think it is an opinion.

1. "Boy!" cried Jenna. "The frontier was sometimes a wild place." _____

2. "That's certainly true," replied Brian. "There were more outlaws on the frontier than law-abiding citizens." _____

3. "But," added Jenna, "most outlaws were decent fellows who went bad. They never hurt innocent people." _____

4. "That's right," said Brian. "Jesse James and other guys even helped widows and old people." _____

5. "Even so," said Jenna, "outlaws who ended up in courts like that of Judge Parker ran the risk of being hanged." _____

6. "Yes," added Brian, "Old Judge Parker strung up almost 90 bad guys in Fort Smith, Arkansas." _____

7. "No," disagreed Jenna. "I heard he hanged three or four hundred before he was through." _____

8. "Well, regardless of the number, his hangings were like a circus," said Brian. "Folks came from miles around to enjoy the show." _____

9. "Talk about a circus," Brian continued, "how about those vigilante committees? They were as bad as the outlaws they hanged—taking the law into their own hands the way they did." _____

10. "Well, I don't know," countered Jenna. "They fulfilled a need at a time when the frontier was in desperate need of law and order." _____

From *Everyday Life: The Frontier* © 1999 Good Year Books.

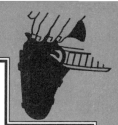

Name _____ Date _____

Think It Through

You have learned that lawlessness was widespread on the frontier. You have also learned that justice was often swift and harsh. Many who ran afoul of the law were hanged without ever having had a trial.

Historians point out that crime prevailed on the frontier because of the absence of law and order. But what about today? We have police forces at every level, but crime remains a major problem. With this thought in mind, respond to the questions.

1. In your opinion, what are some leading causes of crime?

_____

_____

_____

2. Are courts today too lenient on criminals? Give examples.

_____

_____

_____

3. Should youthful offenders be tried as adults? Why or why not?

_____

_____

_____

4. What are your opinions about parole, or the early release of inmates from jail or prison? Should parole be continued or done away with? Why?

_____

_____

_____

5. What are some ways to reduce crime in the United States?

_____

_____

_____

Name _____ Date _____

Write a Letter

Write a letter to James S. Hogg, the Governor of Texas from 1891 to 1896, demanding that Judge Roy Bean be removed from the bench. List reasons why you think he is not worthy of that position and cite imaginary cases supporting your view.

Date_____

The Honorable James S. Hogg
Governor of Texas
Austin, Texas

Dear _____,

_____

_____

_____

_____

_____

_____

_____

_____

_____

_____

_____

_____

_____

_____

Sincerely,

_____

From *Everyday Life: The Frontier* © 1999 Good Year Books.

Name _____ Date _____

Solve a Frontier Justice Puzzle

Across

3. What was discovered in California

6. A word derived from Latin meaning "to watch"

8. Hang without a trial

9. Someone who accompanied a friend to a duel

11. The "hanging judge"

Down

1. Tom Smith was once its marshal.

2. Beat with a whip

4. _____ Francisco

5. An arranged fight with pistols or swords

7. Site of Judge Bean's court

10. Judge Roy _____

11. The Law West of the _____

From Everyday Life: The Frontier ©1999 Good Year Books.

CHAPTER 9

Frontier Towns

Helena,
Montana's
main street as
it appeared
after the Civil
War.

Dodge City. Abilene. Wichita. Ellsworth. Virginia City. Tombstone. These were cow towns or mining towns glamorized in western movies. But more about them later.

Most frontier towns had nothing to do with the cattle or mining industries. The majority were farming communities that served the needs of homesteaders. They were places where farmers could sell their crops and buy supplies. They also provided centers for farm folk to share news and gossip. Men sat around potbellied stoves in general stores and talked politics or told yarns, or stories. Women discussed social happenings and looked over the latest materials and fashions. All the while, big-eyed children drooled over the various candies on display in large jars.

You learned in Chapter 7 that frontier towns were exciting places for visiting farm folk. Something was always happening that made a trip to town a memorable experience. Street performers and patent medicine salesmen provided cheap entertainment. Cowboys, ladies in fancy dresses, and sometimes Native Americans made for interesting gawking as they strolled up and down the town's wooden sidewalks. Just the sounds and bustle of a town were enough to thrill homesteaders. They enjoyed the arrival and departure of the stagecoach or locomotive, speculating as to the destinations of the well-dressed travelers aboard.

A typical frontier town had a main street wide enough to allow wagons and teams of mules and horses to turn around. The dirt street was dusty in dry weather and sheer mud in times of heavy rain. On each side was a raised wooden sidewalk lined with hitching posts. Even under the worst conditions, townsfolk and visitors could avoid trampling in the dust and mud. A problem arose, however, when a person's business required that he or she cross from one side of the street to the other.

Every town had at least a livery stable (for boarding horses), a blacksmith

A wooden
sidewalk in a
frontier town
in Kansas.

From *Everyday Life: The Frontier* © 1999 Good Year Books.

shop, a general store, a hotel, a saloon, and a newspaper. A newspaper was so important that the presses often cranked out the news under a cluster of trees until a permanent building went up. As towns grew and prospered, other kinds of shops and stores appeared. Pictures from the late 1800s show bookstores, banks, dry goods stores, restaurants, meat markets, barber shops, and grocers, to name a few.

Of all the stores in a frontier town, the general store was the most popular. Here settlers could buy everything from sugar and salt to boots and baby carriages. Other items included kerosene lamps, canning jars, shoes, flatirons, and men and women's long johns. Tobacco, coffee, schoolbooks, ammunition, gunpowder, and bottled liquor also lined the shelves. Almost anything a pioneer needed could be found at the general store.

A feature characteristic of almost all stores was the false front. A false front made a building constructed of logs or sod appear more sturdy and imposing than it really was. False fronts were made of lumber and came complete with phony windows. Besides giving stores and shops a more attractive appearance, they served as billboards where owners could display their business title in large letters and advertise their wares. Even after lumber became more accessible, false fronts continued to adorn the buildings of frontier towns.

For townspeople who had no construction skills but lots of money, prefabricated buildings could be purchased through a mail-order catalog. An 1870 catalog of the Lyman Bridges Company of Chicago, Illinois, offered a list of 40 ready-made structures. They ranged from tiny, three-room houses to a large church. A small house could be bought for as little as $350. A schoolhouse cost $1,250 and a sizable railway station $1,300. The large church, which included stained-glass windows and an imposing steeple, could be set up in a town for $5,000. The parts of the prefabricated structures were shipped west in wagons, in boxcars, and on riverboats.

Thousands of frontier towns sprang up in the latter part of the 19th century. Some were built near rivers and railroad junctions. Others started as shipping centers for ore or cattle. Many grew up around mines. Towns that were built near transportation centers usually flourished. Those that developed around mining camps were often abandoned when the ore gave out. These latter communities became the famous "ghost towns" of the West.

Citizens of Wichita, Kansas, pose along the wooden sidewalk of the town's main street.

From *Everyday Life: The Frontier* © 1999 Good Year Books.

Prospective owners rush to claim the best tracts of land in the Cherokee Strip of Oklahoma in 1893. The land rush of that year was one of several that took place after former Indian territory was opened to settlement in 1889.

Sometimes frontier people would establish a town and then discover that the railroad had passed them by. When this happened, did the residents throw up their hands in disgust and give up? No. They simply dismantled the entire town and moved it several miles to intercept the tracks. They transported walls, windows, and even wooden sidewalks to the new site. The twenty six residents of Merna, Kansas, relocated their small town in this way in 1886.

The speed at which a frontier town could spring up was mind-boggling. Bovard, Nevada, consisted of four or five tents on the morning of its first day in existence. By afternoon, its main street was a mile long and lined with tent businesses. When Oklahoma was opened to settlement by the government in 1889 and settlers rushed to claim the best land, the small community of Guthrie had 10,000 inhabitants by the end of the first day! By the end of Guthrie's first week, some tents were being replaced by wooden structures, and the town already had 50 saloons!

To the casual observer, the rush to Guthrie must have been an amusing spectacle. President Benjamin Harrison had declared noon on April 22 as the starting time. Long before that hour, prospective settlers waited at the district line for the appointed time. When a bugle sounded, the race was on. Hundreds of prairie schooners drawn by oxen or mules took off in a tremendous cloud of dust. Settlers without wagons galloped away on horseback, while those with no means of transportation dashed off running at top speed. Those on foot surely chuckled as they were passed by a number of men pedaling along on high-wheeled bicycles and four small-statured circus clowns racing by on the same horse. Six trainloads of land seekers that started last quickly overcame the others and reached Guthrie first. Even before the trains stopped, men jumped from the moving cars and began hammering stakes into lots already marked off by surveyors. And in this most unusual way, the town of Guthrie, Oklahoma, was born.

Although, as previously pointed out, most frontier towns were farming communities, it is mining towns such as Tombstone, Arizona, and the cow towns of Kansas that have been romanticized by the movies. Were towns like Abilene, Wichita, and Dodge City as rough and as bad as Hollywood has made them out to be?

From *Everyday Life: The Frontier* © 1999 Good Year Books.

Yes and no. To be sure, there were brawls and shoot-outs and murders. There were desperadoes and shysters and shady characters aplenty. But statistics show that Hollywood produced more dead badmen than there actually were. In the fifteen years from 1870 to 1885, the five main cattle towns of Kansas had a combined total of only 45 deaths as a result of gunplay. Most towns required that rambunctious cowboys leave their six-shooters at the sheriff's office during their stay.

A large crowd jams the wooden sidewalk in front of the land office in Garden City, Kansas, in 1885.

One reason for depriving cowboys of their guns when they entered a town was to prevent the practice of "hurrahing." After a long cattle drive from Texas, nothing delighted tired and dirty cowboys more than to hurrah a town. This meant they would ride in at top speed, firing their weapons and screaming as loud as they could. Often they rode up and down the wooden sidewalks and right into a hotel or saloon. Sometimes they shot out all the lights and rode their horses across pool tables and other furnishings. Texas cowboys considered hurrahing an excellent way of "blowing off steam." The degree of hurrahing that went on in a town depended on the courage and firmness of the sheriff at the time.

Although gunfights did not occur to the extent Hollywood would have us believe, cow towns nonetheless were wild and rough places. Solid citizens often lived in one part of town while less respectable folk lived in the other. In Abilene, Kansas, for example, law-abiding residents lived north of the railroad tracks, where the majority of the stores, banks, and churches were located. Residents to whom the law meant little lived south of the tracks, where most of the hotels, saloons, and gambling dens could be found.

Cooks, waitresses, and others pose on the steps of a hotel in Wallace, Kansas, in the 1800s. Note the bearded gentleman at the bottom left of the picture with his "six-shooter" at the ready.

Dodge City went one step further than Abilene. It had separate cemeteries for those who obeyed the law and those who did not. Outlaws and other wrongdoers were buried at a graveyard called Boot Hill. Its name came from the fact that most of its occupants died with their boots on.

In time, frontier towns were tamed as law and order prevailed. But frontier folk remained rough and crude in manners. A sign on the wall of a building hosting a dance in Englewood, Kansas, in the 1890s showed an example of this. Printed in large letters was the plea: "Please Don't Spit on the Floor!"

From *Everyday Life: The Frontier* © 1999 Good Year Books.

Name _____ Date _____

Solve Some Cow-Town Math

Here are several math problems having to do with life in a frontier cow town. Space is provided for you to solve each problem. Write your answers on the lines associated with the questions.

1. Sam McCarty of Manhattan, Kansas, purchased a small prefabricated dwelling by mail-order catalog. His three-room house consisted of a kitchen that measured 12' by 10', a living room whose dimensions were 10' by 12', and a bedroom that measured 7' by 12'. What was the total square footage of Sam's house?

   _____ square feet

2. The city of San Francisco, California, had a population of 800 people when the gold rush began in 1849. In six years, this number had increased by an astounding 6150%. What was San Francisco's population in 1855? _____

3. In 1867, 35,000 cattle were shipped from Abilene, Kansas, to the East. This number increased to 75,000 in 1868; went to 350,000 in 1869; fell slightly to 300,000 in 1870; and jumped to 700,000 in 1871. Using these figures, answer these questions.

   a. What was the total number of cattle shipped out in the years from 1867 to 1871? _____ cattle

   b. How many more cattle were processed in 1871 than 1867?

   _____

   c. How many times as many cattle passed through Abilene in 1869 as in 1867? _____

Name _____ Date _____

Improve Your Map Skills

Many famous frontier towns sprang up in Kansas. This was because longhorn cattle from Texas were driven there to meet the railroads that carried them to markets in the East.

Find Kansas on a wall map or in an atlas. Then answer these questions.

1. Kansas is situated almost exactly in the center of the continental United States. North of Kansas is the state of _____. To the south is _____, while _____ is to the east and _____ to the west.

2. Both Dodge City and Wichita are located on the _____ River.

3. To reach Tombstone, Arizona, from Wichita, one would travel in which direction? _____

4. Virginia City, Nevada, another famous frontier town, was located almost due _____ (which direction?) of Manhattan, Kansas.

5. The little town of Abilene, Kansas, is located _____ (which direction?) of the city of Wichita.

6. Of the Kansas cow towns of Dodge City, Abilene, Ellsworth, and Wichita, which became the largest? _____

7. Which city in eastern Kansas lies adjacent to a much larger city of the same name in Missouri? _____

8. The capital of Kansas is _____.

9. To reach San Francisco, California, from the capital of Kansas, a traveler would pass through the states of _____, _____, and _____.

10. Write the capitals of the states that are north, south, east, and west of Kansas. _____
_____
_____
_____

Name _____ Date _____

Write a Letter

Imagine that you have just arrived by stagecoach in a bustling frontier town. You have come West to seek your fortune, and your first impressions of the town will help you determine whether you will stay. As you make your way to your hotel, you take in the sights and sounds of an environment that is exciting but at the same time a little disturbing.

On the lines, write a letter to a friend back East describing your feelings about your new surroundings.

Date _____

Dear _____,

_____

_____

_____

_____

_____

_____

_____

_____

_____

_____

_____

_____

_____

_____

_____

_____

_____

_____

Sincerely,

_____

From Everyday Life: The Frontier © 1999 Good Year Books.

Name _____ Date _____

Create a Frontier-Town Bulletin Board
(A Teacher-directed Activity)

Create a bulletin board display depicting one side of the main street of a frontier town. Assign students to draw and cut out the various stores and shops that might line the street. Other students can sketch and cut out pictures of townspeople, horses, wagons, and perhaps even a stagecoach. Several can draw the street—complete with wooden sidewalks—to which the stores will be stapled or tacked onto whatever paper is chosen to cover the bulletin board.

Before students begin, decide on the dimensions of the stores that are to be drawn so that enough space is available on the bulletin board to accommodate them. With the possible exception of the general store, the hotel, and the church, the stores should be of uniform size.

Most books that deal with the frontier or the West contain pictures showing the kinds of stores characteristic of frontier towns. You can also find some examples in this chapter.

Stores and shops that might be included are

1. general store
2. bank
3. blacksmith shop
4. livery stable
5. hotel
6. saloon
7. barber shop
8. law office
9. drug store
10. restaurant
11. meat market
12. jail
13. church

Materials that will prove useful are

1. bulletin board paper or a comparable piece of meat-wrapping paper
2. magic markers or crayons
3. construction, typing, or copy paper
4. cutout letters for the title of the display
5. scissors
6. rulers
7. glue
8. stapler and staples

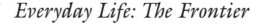

CHAPTER 10

Heroes, Heroines, and Others

The history of the frontier is filled with the stories of fascinating and memorable pioneers. Some were true heroes, while others were ordinary people who led interesting lives. Some, like Daniel Boone, Kit Carson, and Calamity Jane, are practically household names. Others, though not as well known, are just as interesting. They include the likes of Bill Pickett, Nat Love, Stagecoach Mary, and Pearl Hart. This chapter will look briefly at the lives of these and other colorful characters of the frontier era.

Meriwether Lewis and William Clark with Sacajawea in Montana. The explorers' survey of the Louisiana Territory would not have been possible without Sacajawea's services as a guide.

Daniel Boone might be considered America's first frontier hero. He led settlers across the Appalachian Mountains through the Cumberland Gap into what later became the state of Kentucky. He was a renowned hunter, trapper, guide, and Indian fighter. Even though he fought many skirmishes in the wilderness with Indians, he won the respect of many of them for his cunning and bravery. Boone was said to have stated that when he could see the chimney smoke of his nearest neighbor it was time to move on. He eventually ended up in what is now the state of Missouri, where he lived to the age of 86.

Another early frontier hero was Davy Crockett. He served under Andrew Jackson in the Creek War (1813–1814) and later represented Tennessee in the U.S. Congress. In Washington, Crockett went about in leather clothes complete with a squirrel-skin cap. When he was defeated for reelection in 1834, he went to Texas. There he joined the Texas fight for independence from Mexico. In 1836, he and 186 others were killed by a Mexican army while defending the Alamo, a San Antonio mission that had been converted to a fort.

Just as Daniel Boone blazed a trail across the Appalachians, Kit (Christopher) Carson did the same across the Rocky Mountains. In Carson's lifetime, he was a trapper, scout, guide, and Civil War general. In the 1840s he guided a number of expeditions across the mountains to California. Carson never learned to read and write until well into his fifties, but he knew and understood Native Americans better than most people of his times. His diplomacy and actions often helped ease tensions between Indians and whites.

From *Everyday Life: The Frontier* © 1999 GoodYear Books.

The list of early frontier heroes is endless. It also includes pioneers such as Meriwether Lewis, William Clark, and Jim Bridger. But many memorable people of the frontier never made it into the history books, including quite a few black Americans.

In the years following the Civil War, many black Americans went west to seek a better life. Some migrated to Kansas, while others ventured into Indian Territory, later known as Oklahoma. Most were homesteaders who only wanted to carve a living from the land. Others were cowboys and even rodeo performers.

The best known of the black cowboys was Bill Pickett. He is remembered for inventing the rodeo event known as bulldogging, or steer wrestling. Bill had a most unique way of wrestling a steer to the ground. Once he had the animal's horns in a firm grip, he clamped down on its upper lip with his teeth. The fact that he could pull a steer to the ground in that manner suggests that steers not only have sensitive lips but that Bill had an extraordinary set of teeth

Bill Pickett's fame spread far and wide. In 1908, he accepted a challenge to go up against a fierce bull in a ring in Mexico City. He did not have to throw the bull but only hold onto its horns for five seconds. If he succeeded, he would win $5,000. With the Mexicans in attendance cheering for the bull, Pickett entered the ring and went about his task. Although he was gored and received numerous cuts, he held on long enough to pocket the $5,000.

Bill Pickett, a black rodeo performer who invented steer wrestling, or bulldogging. No cowboy ever attempted to duplicate his feat of making a thrown steer flip over by clamping down on its upper lip with his teeth!

Nat Love was another famous black cowboy. He was an ex-slave from Tennessee who went west when he was fifteen. He became a cowboy for $30 a month and drove cattle to Kansas and other points. Once he helped drive a herd from Arizona to Deadwood City, Dakota Territory. He arrived in Deadwood on July 4, 1876, and entered several contests that were part of the town's Independence Day celebration. With relative ease, he won both the roping and shooting competitions. Admiring citizens of Deadwood proclaimed him to be the champion roper of the West.

Mary Fields was also an ex-slave from Tennessee who went west in 1884. She became a legend in the small Montana town of Cascade from 1900–1910. Movie star Gary Cooper remembered her well from when he was a boy growing up in the area. Cooper recalled that Mary was about six feet tall and as tough as any man. She carried a gun under her apron and was always ready

From Everyday Life: The Frontier © 1999 Good Year Books.

for anyone who crossed her. She earned the nickname "Stagecoach Mary" from driving a mail coach for eight years. As an impressionable youngster, Gary Cooper would gaze in awe at the strange lady sitting atop her coach wearing a man's hat and smoking a cigar.

Mary Fields was but one of many women who became a part of the frontier drama. Another, and one of the first, was Sacajawea. Sacajawea was a young Shoshone Indian girl who in 1805 guided Lewis and Clark across the Rocky Mountains to the Pacific. With her help, the vast region acquired in the Louisiana Purchase was explored and mapped.

Sacajawea was well suited to lead Lewis and Clark on their expedition. A few years before, she had been captured by enemy Indians and sold to a French trader named Toussaint Charbonneau. The very territory in which the explorers needed a guide was the homeland from which Sacajawea had been taken.

A later famous frontierswoman was Calamity Jane, whose real name was Martha Jane Canary. She was called "Calamity" because she supposedly warned men that a calamity would be their lot if they offended her.

Calamity Jane was a skilled rider and an expert with a rifle and revolver. She drifted throughout the West, working at jobs usually reserved for men. She wore men's clothes, chewed tobacco, and frequented saloons. But to the people of Deadwood, South Dakota, she was a heroine. When a smallpox epidemic broke out in 1875, Calamity stayed and nursed many miners back to health. In so doing, she put her own life in jeopardy. When she died in 1903, grateful townspeople gave Calamity Jane the largest funeral in the history of Deadwood.

You may be familiar with Annie Oakley. Annie was a farm girl from the backwoods of Ohio who gained fame as a member of Buffalo Bill's Wild West Show. Her real name was Phoebe Ann Oakley Mozee.

When Annie was only nine, she became a crack shot with a rifle. For several years, she helped support her family by shooting and selling rabbits and game. When she was fifteen, she entered a shooting contest in Cincinnati. She married the marksperson she bested in the competition, and they both joined Buffalo Bill's show in 1885.

Annie Oakley, called "Little Sure Shot" because of her skill with a rifle. Annie, whose real name was Phoebe Ann Oakley Mozee, toured the United States and Europe with Buffalo Bill's Wild West Show.

From *Everyday Life: The Frontier* © 1999 Good Year Books.

For seventeen years Annie Oakley thrilled audiences both in America and Europe. She was so skilled with a rifle that she once shot a cigarette from the mouth of the Kaiser of Germany. Each time a playing card was tossed into the air, she could shoot four or five holes in it before it hit the ground. And sitting astride a galloping horse, she could hit 999 out of 1,000 glass objects thrown into the air. Small wonder that everyone called her "Little Sure-Shot"!

Another well-known frontier figure who joined Buffalo Bill's show was the great Sioux chief Sitting Bull. Sitting Bull was one of the Indian leaders who defeated General George Custer at the Battle of Little Bighorn in Montana in 1876. Afterward, he fled to Canada but later returned when he received a presidential pardon.

Like Annie Oakley, Sitting Bull toured the world with the Wild West show. Some people thought performing in such a way was a comedown for the great leader, but Sitting Bull did not see it that way. He frankly stated that he accepted Buffalo Bill's offer because he needed the money. While with the show, Sitting Bull made Annie Oakley a Sioux "princess" and literally adopted her as his daughter. He is credited with giving her the nickname "Wan-tan-yeya Ci-sci-la," which in the Sioux language means "Little Sure-Shot."

Some frontier folk heroes ran afoul of the law. One was Pearl Hart. Pearl was fifteen years old when, while dressed as a boy, she committed the last stagecoach robbery on the frontier. She ultimately served five years in the Yuma Territorial Prison for her misdeed.

Another lawbreaker was Isom Dart. Isom was a good-natured cowboy who apparently never did anyone harm. But Isom had a serious flaw: he could not resist on occasion taking a cow or two that belonged to someone else. Isom tried many times to go straight, but the temptation of rustling always got the better of him. He was shot dead from an ambush by a bounty hunter in 1900.

Finally, there were the "bad guys" of the western frontier—outlaws such as Billy the Kid, Jesse James, Cherokee Bill, and the Dalton Gang. Contrary to what legends and Hollywood producers would have us believe, there is no evidence showing that any of these criminals ever stooped to help a needy widow or give a dime to the poor. They were cold-blooded killers who cared nothing for the welfare of other people. Most were illiterate, and some were considered to have a mental age of an eight- to twelve-year-old.

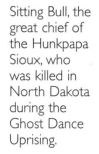

Sitting Bull, the great chief of the Hunkpapa Sioux, who was killed in North Dakota during the Ghost Dance Uprising.

From *Everyday Life: The Frontier* © 1999 Good Year Books.

Name _____ Date _____

Name That Frontier Person

As is true of any period of history, the frontier era produced a number of interesting and fascinating people. Twelve of these are listed in the word box below. Select the correct name from the box and write it on the blank line in front of each statement.

Daniel Boone

Sitting Bull

Kit Carson

Davy Crockett

Isom Dart

Mary Fields

Pearl Hart

Calamity Jane

Nat Love

Annie Oakley

Bill Pickett

1. _____ "I drove a mail coach in Cascade, Montana."

2. _____ "I led pioneers through the Cumberland Gap to Kentucky."

3. _____ "I committed the last stagecoach robbery on the frontier."

4. _____ "My real name was Martha Jane Canary."

5. _____ "I was a Sioux chief who joined Buffalo Bill's Wild West Show."

6. _____ "I guided Lewis and Clark across the Rockies."

7. _____ "I was a rustler who never succeeded at going straight."

8. _____ "The people of Deadwood proclaimed me the champion roper of the West."

9. _____ "I was one of the defenders of the Alamo."

10. _____ "I invented the rodeo event of bulldogging."

11. _____ "I was called 'Little Sure-Shot.'"

12. _____ "My real first name was Christopher."

From *Everyday Life: The Frontier* ©1999 Good Year Books.

Name _____ Date _____

Complete a Vocabulary Exercise

Select the meaning of each word as it is used in Chapter 10. The number of the paragraph from which the word is taken is in parentheses beside it. Write the letter of the correct choice on the line to the left.

_____ 1. **colorful** (paragraph 1)
(a) vivid
(b) full of color
(c) interesting or different

_____ 2. **state** (paragraph 2)
(a) one of the smaller parts of a nation
(b) a condition of mind or feeling
(c) say

_____ 3. **mission** (paragraph 3)
(a) duty or purpose
(b) church
(c) group sent on some special business

_____ 4. **carve** (paragraph 6)
(a) achieve by effort or ability
(b) cut into slices or pieces
(c) make by cutting

_____ 5. **drive** (paragraph 9)
(a) trip in an automobile
(b) make go where one wishes
(c) energy

_____ 6. **legend** (paragraph 10)
(a) words that are part of a picture or diagram
(b) what is written on a coin or medal
(c) person who inspires stories or tales

_____ 7. **crossed** (paragraph 10)
(a) met and passed
(b) drew a line across
(c) opposed or bothered

_____ 8. **coach** (paragraph 10)
(a) teach or train
(b) person who trains athletic teams
(c) closed carriage pulled by horse

_____ 9. **lot** (paragraph 13)
(a) fate or condition
(b) plot of ground
(c) collection

_____ 10. **crack** (paragraph 16)
(a) excellent
(b) split or opening
(c) sudden, sharp noise

_____ 11. **game** (paragraph 16)
(a) contest
(b) wild animals hunted for food or sport
(c) brave

_____ 12. **producer** (paragraph 22)
(a) person who grows or manufactures things that are used by others
(b) person who finances and supervises a play or some other form of public entertainment
(c) a person who turns out an extraordinary amount of work

Name _____ Date _____

Distinguish Between Fact and Opinion

Remembering that a fact is something that can be proven while an opinion is only a strong belief, decide which term fits each of the statements.

Write "F" if you think a sentence is a fact. Write "O" if you consider it only an opinion.

1. Calamity Jane was the toughest person on the frontier.

2. Annie Oakley was a skilled marksperson.

3. Daniel Boone preferred not to have neighbors close by.

4. Daniel Boone knew more about Native Americans than any person of his day.

5. Hollywood movies often present an unreal picture of life on the frontier.

6. Davy Crockett was once a U.S. Congressman.

7. Bill Pickett could wrestle a steer to the ground using only his teeth.

8. Bill Pickett was the best steer wrestler who ever lived.

9. Everybody in Cascade, Montana, looked up to Stagecoach Mary.

10. Sacajawea helped guide Lewis and Clark through the Rocky Mountains.

11. Sitting Bull disgraced Native Americans everywhere by agreeing to perform in Buffalo Bill's Wild West Show.

12. Kit Carson showed understanding toward Native Americans and got along well with those he met.

13. Most black Americans who went west were interested in farming.

14. Most frontier people viewed outlaws as folk heroes.

15. Nat Love was a champion roper and marksperson.

Name _____ Date _____

Think It Through

In Chapter 10, you read about a number of men and women who were a part of the frontier saga. Some were good, while others were bad. Some could even be considered heroes.

How are heroes identified? With this thought in mind, respond to the questions.

1. In your opinion, what are the characteristics of a true hero?

    _____

    _____

    _____

2. What person(s) mentioned in Chapter 10 fulfills your requirements of a hero? Why?

    _____

    _____

    _____

    _____

    _____

3. Name several persons today you consider heroes, and explain why.

    _____

    _____

    _____

    _____

    _____

4. Are frontier people—good and bad—depicted more accurately on television and in the movies today than they previously were? If so, in what way(s)?

    _____

    _____

    _____

    _____

CHAPTER II

Native Americans and the Frontier

The history of the frontier is more than just a story of homesteaders, miners, cowboys, and others. It is also the story of the final years of freedom for the American Indian.

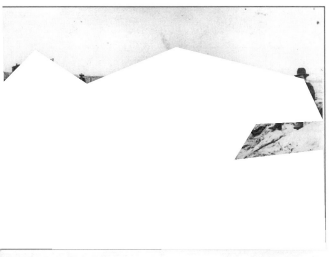

A man sits atop a pile of buffalo hides in Dodge City, Kansas, in 1874. Buffalo hunters took only the hides, leaving the meat to rot on the plains.

When Europeans began to colonize North America in the early 1600s, there were perhaps one million Native Americans living from the Rio Grande River in the south to Canada in the north. They were separated into numerous tribes and bands and spoke many different languages. Some lived in established communities where they farmed or fished. Others were hunters who lived in portable tepees and followed buffalo and other game wherever they went. All cherished a simple way of life that was both unappreciated and misunderstood by European settlers.

In spite of their differences, the Indians of North America shared many common beliefs. One of the most important was their view of the Earth. Native Americans believed that the Earth was their mother, to be shared and enjoyed by all. As such, it could not be bought and sold and divided into sections in the manner of white settlers. It could be farmed and hunted and even fought over, but it could never be parceled out into individual lots. All living things, including animals, were entitled to share in this gift from "the Great Spirit."

Animals were respected by Native Americans and looked upon as their brothers. No animal was ever killed simply for sport. Native Americans hunted to live and to obtain the other necessities of life.

Probably the best example of the relationship between Native Americans and animals is the buffalo. On the Great Plains, this cowlike animal was the basis of life for the Indians there. Unlike white hunters who took only the skins and sometimes the tongues, Indians made use of every part of the buffalo. The meat was the staple of their diet. The skin was used to make clothes and tepees. Horns and bones were shaped into tools and weapons. Entrails were used to make bowstrings. Dung was the fuel source for their fires. Nothing was wasted.

From Everyday Life: The Frontier © 1999 Good Year Books.

The Indians of North America also held common beliefs concerning family life and children. Boys and girls from an early age learned to remain silent and respectful in the presence of their elders. They were almost never punished physically for any wrongdoing. They were praised when they were good and shamed when they were not. A stern look from a parent was usually enough to bring an unruly child into line.

Native American men spent their time hunting and fighting. They seldom helped with what was considered "women's work." This even included such tasks as putting up and taking down the family's shelter and packing belongings when the tribe moved to a different place. These strenuous jobs always fell to the women.

Women were also responsible for cooking, sewing, preparing hides, and taking care of children. Even so, their work was never considered lowly and unimportant. They would have been just as embarrassed doing the work of men as men would have been performing their tasks. To the Native American, all work was thought to be noble and worthwhile.

Young Indians learned the skills and customs of their tribe from their parents, grandparents, and relatives. Boys learned to hunt, trap, and fish. They also were instructed in making bows and arrows and fashioning canoes from the bark of trees. Girls watched their mothers and learned to sew and cook. They also acquired skills in making baskets, pottery, and blankets. By observing and imitating their parents, Indian boys and girls learned in much the same way as the children of the pioneers.

In the beginning, Native Americans were friendly toward the English and others who came to their shores. They taught the newcomers how to grow food and how to survive in the wilderness. They saw little reason to fear a handful of white settlers from across the sea. After all, America was a large continent. There was plenty of room for everyone.

Friendly relations, however, soon soured. As the eastern seaboard began to fill up with colonists, many English settlers began to turn their eyes west to new lands beyond the Appalachian Mountains. Native Americans viewed this desire for expansion as a threat to their existence, and confrontations between the cultures arose.

You will remember that King George III of Great Britain, to maintain peace, finally forbade settlement west of the Allegheny Mountains, a range of the Appalachians. His order was the famous Proclamation of 1763. But issuing a proclamation and enforcing it are two different things. With the

An 1876 advertisement for buffalo robes. The variety of products offered for sale points to the huge demand for goods made from buffalo hides.

From Everyday Life: The Frontier © 1999 Good Year Books.

King miles away in England, colonists ignored the decree and began to push across the mountains.

Indians of the Cherokee nation being forcibly relocated to Indian Territory (Oklahoma) in 1838. One-fourth of the Cherokees died along the way. From a painting by Robert Lindneux.

When the colonists proclaimed their independence from England in 1776, the fate of Native Americans was sealed. The new American government began to set aside reservations for Indians as early as 1786. Then, in 1830, the Indian Removal Act was passed. This act provided for the removal of the Indian populations of Georgia and the Gulf states to Oklahoma. Why was this done? The answer is simple. White settlers wanted the land on which the Indians had become successful farmers and citizens. Although many Indians had intermarried with whites and had adopted white ways, they too were told to move.

The removal of the Indians began in 1831. First the Choctaws were led away, followed in turn by the Creeks, the Chickasaws, the Cherokees, and finally the Seminoles. But the Seminoles did not leave without a fight. They carried out a long and costly war with the United States government. When the fighting ended in 1842, they too, except for a small group which retreated to the Everglades and never officially made peace with the United States, were marched westward to Oklahoma.

Thousands of Native Americans who departed for Oklahoma never made it. They died along the way from hunger, disease, and exposure. Many more perished after reaching their destination from epidemics and attacks by warlike Western tribes who already lived there. Small wonder that this shameful period in our nation's history was afterward referred to by the Indians as the "Trail of Tears."

By the 1840s, time was running out for America's Indians. Earlier, war and disease had wiped out the Eastern tribes. Now the forced march to Oklahoma had removed those from the South. What was left of the Indian population was squeezed into an area that grew smaller as each year passed.

Whereas Indian "wars" had occurred from time to time before pioneers began to push across the Great Plains to the Pacific, they occurred with greater frequency after the Civil War. Between 1869 and 1876, more than 200 pitched battles were fought. While the Indians won some of these engagements, they had no hope of holding off the relentless advance of white civilization.

From *Everyday Life: The Frontier* © 1999 Good Year Books.

Most Americans believed it was the destiny of the United States to expand to the Pacific. Native Americans were considered a hindrance to such expansion, and therefore the expansion-minded pioneers felt they had to be eliminated. One way of ridding the plains of Indians was to kill off the buffalo. From 1865 to 1884, white hunters shot and killed buffalo in ever-increasing numbers. They killed only for the furs, leaving the carcasses to rot on the plains. Some killed only for sport. Trains crossing the prairie sometimes stopped to allow hunters with powerful rifles to shoot buffalo. In 1872–1873 alone, white hunters shot more than 1,250,000 of these majestic animals. By the next year 3,000,000 buffalo a year were being killed.

Cheyennes destroy a portion of Union Pacific railroad tracks to disrupt its construction in May 1867.

With the slaughter of the buffalo, the way of life of the Plains Indians came to an end. An attempt was made to turn Native Americans into farmers, but, in general, this effort failed. Some Plains tribes were reduced to eating dogs and coyotes—and even their own ponies.

In desperation, a small number of Indians turned to what came to be called the Religion of the Ghost Dance. They believed if they performed this dance, miraculous things would happen: the buffalo would return, and past heroes and loved ones would rise from the grave. Perhaps the earth would be reborn and the white man plowed under the soil. This new religion was preached by a Paiute medicine man named Wovoka, who also taught that special ghost shirts would protect believers from the bullets of the white man.

Plains Indians performing the Ghost Dance on a reservation some time between 1888 and 1890.

The Religion of the Ghost Dance spread new fear among the whites of the plains and led to the final "battle" between Native Americans and soldiers of the United State Army. This last battle will be discussed in more detail in the Epilogue, p. 90.

Name _____ Date _____

Suppose History Had Been Different

King George III of Great Britain issued the Proclamation of 1763 to keep the peace with the Indians. The proclamation banned white settlement west of the Allegheny Mountains. For the most part, the order was ignored and colonists pushed on across the mountains in search of better land.

But suppose the British government had rigidly enforced the proclamation. Suppose colonists had remained content to stay along the Atlantic seaboard and never venture into lands occupied by the Indians.

On the lines, write how you think the history of America might have turned out differently if the above scenario had actually happened.

_____
_____
_____
_____
_____
_____
_____
_____
_____
_____
_____
_____
_____
_____
_____
_____
_____
_____
_____
_____
_____
_____
_____

Name _____ Date _____

Write a Letter

Suppose you were living when the Indian Removal Act was passed in 1830. Write a letter to President Andrew Jackson expressing your displeasure and anger at the forced removal of the southern Indian tribes to Oklahoma. Give reasons why you consider such action unfair.

Date_____

The President
The White House
Washington, D.C.

Dear Mr. President:

_____

_____

_____

_____

_____

_____

_____

_____

_____

_____

_____

_____

_____

_____

_____

Sincerely,

_____

From *Everyday Life: The Frontier* ©1999 Good Year Books.

Name _____ Date _____

Compare Buffaloes and Bison

You may be surprised to learn that the animal the Plains Indians depended on for their very existence was not really a buffalo. It was actually a bison.

Are buffaloes and bison basically the same? Or are there definite differences between the two? Research buffaloes and bison in an encyclopedia or other book. Then answer the questions.

1. How do buffaloes and bison differ in appearance?

_____

_____

_____

_____

2. In what ways are buffaloes and bison similar?

_____

_____

_____

3. In what areas of the world are buffaloes found in the wild, and how are they useful to the people who live there?

_____

_____

_____

4. List several different kinds of buffaloes.

_____

_____

5. Although laws were eventually passed to protect bison, they are still today considered an endangered species. What does *endangered species* mean?

_____

_____

From *Everyday Life: The Frontier* © 1999 Good Year Books.

Epilogue

By the year 1890, all available land on the Great Plains had been claimed. Cattlemen, who had driven the Indians from the region, were in turn replaced by homesteaders. Land was fenced in with barbed wire, and windmills drew precious water from the ground to fertilize crops. Railroads brought thousands of European immigrants from the East to join those farmers already there. In a relatively short time, the Plains filled up with settlers.

The fencing-in of the open range was one of two significant events marking the end of the frontier. The other was the last major encounter to occur between whites and Native Americans in North America. This encounter, which ended in the massacre of hundreds of innocent people, took place at a creek called Wounded Knee in South Dakota on December 29, 1890.

Mention was made in Chapter 11 of the Ghost Dance and how it led some whites to believe an Indian uprising was in the making. Thinking such, soldiers from the Seventh U.S. Cavalry were sent to disarm a group of 356 Sioux under the leadership of Chief Big Foot. The Sioux were on their way back to the reservation at Pine Ridge, South Dakota, and had no plans to attack anyone. More than 200 in the group were women and children.

An advertisement offering free homes and cheap land in South Dakota on a site of the former Sioux reservation.

When the soldiers caught up with the Indians, a scuffle broke out. Before it was over, nearly 300 (by some counts) of the Sioux lay dead in the snow. Many of these were women and children mowed down as they attempted to run away. In this disgraceful manner, the United States Army brought peace to the Plains.

With the end of the open range and the final "defeat" of the Indians, an era in American history came to an end. The frontier was no more.

Answers to Activities

Chapter 1

Interpret a Bar Graph

1. 2,160 miles   2. 432 miles
3. 740 miles   4. No   5. 10 times
6. 500 miles

Chapter 2

Fill in a Venn Diagram

Answers will vary but might include
the following:

Log Cabin–made of logs 12 to 18 feet
long; logs notched on ends; some
had puncheon floors; cracks
between logs were chinked; roof
of overlapping shingles

Sod House–made of blocks of sod;
cozy and warm in winter; cool in
summer; damp, musty, and leaky

Both–small; sparsely furnished;
inexpensive to build; meant to be
a temporary home

Use Context Clues to Complete Sentences

lived; intended; built; felled; cut;
notched; fit; left; laid; called; satisfied;
required; hauled; stacked; lacked;
persevered; tamed; enjoyed

Chapter 3

Solve a Clothing Puzzle

Across–1. cap   2. calico   5. woolsey
7. Levis   8. bandanna   10. spurs
11. gallon

Down–1. chaps   3. boots   4. moccasin
6. flax   9. deerskin

Solve Some Cowboy Math Problems

1. $18.75; $11.25   2. $115.00
3. 6

Find the Main Idea

Paragraph 2–Corn was the staple
crop of pioneers.

Paragraph 5–Salt was scarce on the
frontier.

Paragraph 8–Many foods were
preserved for future use.

Paragraph 11–Early pioneers copied
the dress of Indians.

Paragraph 14–Miners and cowboys
wore "store bought" clothes.

Paragraph 16–Boots were important
to a cowboy.

Details Supporting the Main Idea of
Paragraph 6–Pioneers used honey
and syrup for sweeteners; they
made coffee from sassafras root or
from parched corn and barley

Chapter 4

Solve Some Chore-Related Math

1. mode 3;   median 5
2. range 7;   mean 5

Chapter 5

Complete a Vocabulary Exercise

1. b   2. c   3. b   4. a   5. b
6. a   7. b   8. c

From Everyday Life: The Frontier © 1999 Good Year Books.

Chapter 6

Interpret a Bar Graph

1. 107   2. 25%   3. 7%   4. 18
5. 19   6. No

Use Your Critical Thinking Skills

Answers will vary but should be similar to the following:

1. Mary may lose her interest in art because she cannot receive the individual attention she needs.
2. The bullies will probably beat up the smaller boys.
3. Joshua will probably never attend school again.
4. Because of fewer students, Ms. Clay will be able to give more individual attention to each student.

Chapter 7

Solve Some Square Dance Word Problems

1. 1 hour, 15 minutes
2. 0 hours, 25 minutes
3. 20 hours, 30 minutes

Chapter 8

Distinguish Between Fact and Opinion

1. F   2. O   3. O   4. O   5. F
6. F   7. O   8. F   9. O   10. F

Solve a Frontier Justice Puzzle

Across—3. gold   6. vigilante
8. lynch   9. second   11. Parker
Down—1. Abilene   2. flog   4. San
5. duel   7. Langtry   10. Bean
11. Pecos

Chapter 9

Solve Some Cow-Town Math

1. 324 square feet   2. 50,000
3a. 1,460,000   3b. 665,000
3c. 10

Improve Your Map Skills

1. Nebraska, Oklahoma, Missouri, Colorado
2. Arkansas
3. southwest
4. west
5. north
6. Wichita
7. Kansas City
8. Topeka
9. Colorado, Utah, and Nevada
10. Lincoln, Oklahoma City, Jefferson City, Denver

Chapter 10

Name That Frontier Person

1. Mary Fields   7. Isom Dart
2. Daniel Boone   8. Nat Love
3. Pearl Hart   9. Davy Crockett
4. Calamity Jane   10. Bill Pickett
5. Sitting Bull   11. Annie Oakley
6. Sacajawea   12. Kit Carson

Complete a Vocabulary Exercise

1. c   2. a   3. b   4. a   5. b
6. c   7. c   8. c   9. a   10. a
11. b   12. b

Distinguish Between Fact and Opinion

1. O   2. F   3. F   4. O   5. F
6. F   7. F   8. O   9. O   10. F
11. O   12. F   13. F   14. O   15. F

From Everyday Life: The Frontier © 1999 Good Year Books.

Chapter 11

Compare Buffaloes and Bison

Answers will vary, but should include some of the following facts:

1. Buffaloes—look like oxen but have big, sweeping horns; have thirteen pairs of ribs
   Bison—shaggy; have thick manes of hair over their neck, shoulders, and front legs; have a hump of fat on the shoulders; have fourteen pairs of ribs

2. Both have horns and feet with two hooves; both eat plants.

3. They are found in Asia and Africa. They pull plows and do other heavy work. They also provide milk, meat, and hides for the people in those areas.

4. Asian water buffalo, African Cape buffalo, forest buffalo, carabao, pygmy buffalo

5. It means they are in danger of becoming extinct.

Additional Resources

Books for Children

Alter, Judith. *Growing Up in the Old West.* New York: Franklin Watts, 1989.

Alter, Judith. *Women of the Old West.* New York: Franklin Watts, 1989.

Bial, Raymond. *Frontier Home.* Boston: Houghton Mifflin Company, 1993.

Freedman, Russell. *Children of the Wild West.* New York: Clarion Books, 1983.

Matthews, Leonard J. *Pioneers.* Vero Beach, Florida: Rourke Publications, 1989.

Newark, Peter. *Pioneers.* New York: Gallery Books, 1984.

Books for Adults

Barnard, Edward S., ed. *Story of the Great American West.* Pleasantville, New York: Reader's Digest Association, 1977.

Katz, William Loren. *The Black West.* Garden City, New York: Anchor Press/Doubleday, 1973.

Lavender, David. *The American Heritage History of the West.* New York: American Heritage Publishing Company, 1965.

Wheeler, Keith, and the editors of Time-Life Books. *The Townsmen.* New York: Time-Life Books, 1975.

Wright, Louis B. *Everyday Life on the American Frontier.* New York: G. P. Putnam's Sons, 1968.